T0054024

EDITOR'S LETTER

The Qatar conundrum

The World Cup is shining a spotlight on the role of football in the rights landscape, but it's complicated writes **JEMIMAH STEINFELD**

ON A TUESDAY afternoon in November 1945, the streets of Fulham, London filled with people all heading to Stamford Bridge. They were there to see Chelsea FC play Dynamo Moscow and the atmosphere was electric. Cheering crowds bought toffee apples sold by local residents and those without tickets climbed onto the stadium roof to watch. The match didn't disappoint, ending on a thrilling 3-3 draw. It was the start of Dynamo Moscow's UK tour, a tour that has gone down in the books as a huge success. Stalin was delighted. He saw it as a signifier of Communist strength, soft power working at its finest. It was, in short, sportswashing 1945 style.

Sportswashing in 2022 is a similar beast, just on a grander scale, and Qatar, the host of the World Cup in November and December, is its current posterchild. Here's a nation that prohibits homosexuality, has no free press, forbids protest, restricts free speech. It has stadiums built using migrant labour with little to no workers' rights. And yet come November these stadiums will open to the world, international dignitaries will be wined and dined and Qatar will revel in the glory associated with hosting a World Cup.

George Orwell was sickened by the fanfare surrounding Dynamo Moscow in 1945. It was this spectacle that led him to famously describe international sporting events as "mimic warfare" and "orgies of hatred". Should we be sickened too? This was the starting point of our special report. We set out with a simple question: "Is football bad for free speech?" And yet the answer was complex. Kaya Genç, for example, writes about Turkish President Reccep Erdoğan buying up sporting clubs to stop the arenas being used for protest; China's leader Xi Jinping force-feeds the nation's kids a diet of soccer while Uyghur footballers playing for Chinese teams are paraded as examples of racial harmony. But against these negatives were stories of remarkable positivity. Permi Jhooti, the real-life inspiration for Bend It Like Beckham, says football gave her a voice to challenge the traditions she had been raised in. The same applied to Khalida Popal, the first captain of Afghanistan's women's team.

We asked a leading philosopher, Julian Baggini, whether we should expect the world's footballers to speak out against atrocities. His answer was no. We asked an activist from Qatar whether we should boycott the tournament. His answer was yes.

Football is both a beautiful game and an ugly game, all depending on where you are standing. Ask two football fans their verdict on a match and you will get at least three opinions. And interestingly, football is also often a lens through which a nation reveals itself. Hence, in this issue we look at the state of free expression across the world, from the pitch-side up. ✖

Jemimah Steinfeld is Index editor-in-chief

51(03):1/1|DOI:10.1177/03064220221126384

> ## George Orwell was sickened by the fanfare surrounding Dynamo Moscow

---

A cup half full

MARK FRARY introduces our cover artist FATIMA WOJOHAT

Fatima Wojohat was 19 when the Taliban retook Afghanistan. After the Taliban imposed restrictions on women, she started creating artwork on her smartphone.

Her illustration focuses on issues surrounding Qatar's hosting of the World Cup, including the suppression of workers' and women's rights.

There is hope though. She says, "The purpose of drawing hearts in my artworks is to be a light in the darkness."

CONTENTS

Up Front

1   THE QATAR CONUNDRUM:
JEMIMAH STEINFELD
The World Cup is
throwing up questions

4   THE INDEX: MARK FRARY
The latest in the world of
freedom of expression, with
internet shutdowns and
Salman Rushdie's attack in
the spotlight. Plus George M.
Johnson on being banned

Features

14   AN UNHOLY WAR ON
SPEECH: SARAH MYERS
A woman sits on death
row in Pakistan. Her crime?
Saying she was a prophet

17   PERFECTING THE
ART OF OPPRESSION:
MARTHA OTWINOWSKI
Poland's art scene is the latest
victim of nasty politics

21   POLAND'S REDEMPTION
SONGS: MARTIN BRIGHT
In anti apartheid solidarity, reggae
rode with revolution in Europe

24   FIGHTING BACK AGAINST
VENDETTA POLITICS:
HANAN ZAFFAR,
HAMAAD HABIBULLAH
In India, tackling fake news
can land you in a cell

27   THE MAFIA STATE THAT IS
PUTTY IN PUTIN'S HANDS:
MARK SEACOMBE
The truth behind the
spread of pro-Russian
propaganda in Bulgaria

30   BODIES OF EVIDENCE:
SARAH SANDS
A new frontier of journalism
with echoes of a crime-
scene investigator

33   KEEPING THE FAITH:
JEMIMAH STEINFELD

An interview with Benedict
Rogers on challenging Beijing

36   THE DOUBLE CLOSET:
FLO MARKS
Exploring the rampant bi-
phobia that pushes many
to silence their sexuality

40   IS THERE A (REAL) DOCTOR
IN THE HOUSE?: JOHN LLOYD
One journalist uncovers
the secret of Romania's
doctored doctorates

42   THE MICE HEAR THE WORDS
OF THE NIGHT: JIHYUN PARK
A schooling in free
expression, where the
classroom is North Korea

44   THE MOST DANGEROUS
MAN IN GUANTANAMO:
KATIE DANCEY-DOWNS
After years in Guantanamo,
a journalist dedicates himself
to protecting others

47   AMERICA'S COOLEST
MEMBERS CLUB:
OLIVIA SKLENKA
Meet the people fighting against
the surge in book bans

Special Report:
The beautiful game?

50   VICTIM OF ITS
OWN SUCCESS?:
SIMON BARNES
Blame the populists,
not the game

53   STADIUMS BUILT
ON SUFFERING:
ABDULLAH AL-MALIKI
Underneath the suds of
Qatar's sportswashing,
fear and terror remain

56   FOOTBALL'S LEAVING HOME:
KATIE DANCEY-DOWNS
Khalida Popal put women on
the pitch in Afghanistan, before
leading their evacuation

58   EXPOSING SAUDI'S NASTY
TACTICS: ADAM CRAFTON

A sports journalist is forced
into defence after tackling
Saudi Arabia's homophobia

60   IT'S FOUL PLAY IN KASHMIR:
BILAL AHMAD PANDOW
Protest and politically motivated
matches are entwined in
Kashmir's football history

63   HOW 'INDUSTRIAL
FOOTBALL' WAS USED TO
SILENCE PROTESTS:
KAYA GENÇ
Political football: how to
bend it like Erdoğan

67   XI'S REAL CHINA DREAM:
JONATHAN SULLIVAN

While freedoms are
squeezed, China's leader has
a World Cup-sized dream

70 TACKLING ISRAEL'S THORNY
POLITICS: DANIELLA PELED
Can an Arab-majority team
in the Israeli league carve out
a space for free expression?

72 THE STENCH OF WHITE
ELEPHANTS: JAMIL CHADE
Brazil's World Cup swung
open Pandora's Box

74 THE REAL GAME IS POLITICS:
ISSA SIKITI DA SILVA
Is politics welcome on
the pitch in Kenya?

Comment

78 REFEREEING RIGHTS:
JULIAN BAGGINI
Why we shouldn't expect
footballers to hand out
human rights red cards

80 THE OTHER HALF:
PERMI JHOOTI
The real-life inspiration behind
Bend It like Beckham holds up
a mirror to her experience

82 WE DON'T LIKE IT – NO
ONE CARES: MARK GLANVILLE
English football has moved
away from listening to its fans
argues this Millwall supporter

83 MUCH ADO ABOUT
CRITICS: LYN GARDNER
A theatre objects to an
offensive Legally Blonde review

84 ON REPUTATION
LAUNDERING: RUTH SMEETH
Beware those who want to
control their own narrative

Culture

88 THE SOUL OF SUDAN:
STELLA GAITANO,
KATIE DANCEY-DOWNS
What does it mean for deep-
running connections when
you're forced to leave? Censored
writer Stella Gaitano introduces
a new translation of her work

92 MOVING THE GOALPOSTS:
KAYA GENÇ, GUILHERME OSINSKI
Football and politics are
a match made in Turkey.
Kaya Genç fictionalises
an unforgettable game

96 AWAY FROM THE SATANIC:
MALISE RUTHVEN
The leading expert on
Salman Rushdie writes
about an emerging liberalism
in Islamic discourse

CREDIT: Fatima Wojohat

The Index

51(03):4/12|DOI:10.1177/03064220221126385

A round-up of events in the world of free expression from Index's unparalleled network of writers and activists

Edited by
MARK FRARY

PICTURED: Sudanese women take to the streets of the capital Khartoum in July, as they join the ongoing protests against military rule. Army chief Abdel Fattah al-Burhan seized power in a coup in October 2021 and the protests have been deadly, with at least 10 people killed

The Index

ELECTION WATCH

GUILHERME OSINSKI looks at what is happening at the poll booths of the world

1. Brazil

OCTOBER

As Brazil's presidential elections approach, so do fears about the country's future. The two frontrunners in the fight for the presidential seat are current President Jair Bolsonaro (Liberal Party) and his main opponent, Luís Inácio Lula da Silva (Workers' Party), who was president between 2003 and 2010.

Opinion polls show that Lula is in the lead, leading Bolsonaro to question electoral transparency and the likelihood of fraud in the Brazilian system. On 18 July, Bolsonaro invited ambassadors from more than 30 countries to a meeting in which he cast doubt on the credibility of the machines and even suggested the participation of the military to "guarantee safe elections". The day after this meeting, the US embassy in Brasília released a statement supporting Brazilian institutions and describing the electoral system in Brazil as a "model for the world".

Bolsonaro and his sons have disputed approximately 20 elections since 1996, the year the machines were introduced, despite being elected in 19 of them. This has raised concerns that Bolsonaro is attempting to discredit the poll, and may even be planning a coup if defeated.

The election is also seeing an increase in political crime. On 9 July, municipal guard and Workers' Party treasurer Marcelo Arruda was shot dead by federal prison guard Jorge Guaranho, a supporter of Jair Bolsonaro. Back in 2018, Bolsonaro had suggested "shooting the *petralhada*" (referring to people on the left-wing).

2. Slovenia

23 OCTOBER

In October, people in Slovenia will head to the polls to choose their president for the next five years.

Leading the polls is Nataša Pirc Musar, an independent lawyer and journalist who has worked for Melania Trump in the USA. Her supporters hope she can heal the divided country. If she succeeds, it will be the first woman in charge of the country.

Facing Musar is Anže Logar from the right-wing Slovenian Democratic Party, the same party as the country's former Prime Minister Janez Janša.

Logar worked as minister of foreign affairs from March 2020 to June 2022 and during his term, he said that all media outlets in the country belonged to the communist regime. Media freedom in Slovenia has recently been in decline, with journalists, particularly women, being frequently harassed and threatened by politicians, including Janša.

3. Israel

1 NOVEMBER

Israel's legislative elections in November will choose the members of the 25th Knesset. The previous legislative elections in March 2021 produced a hung parliament with neither Benjamin Netanyahu's right-wing bloc or the opposition with enough seats to have a majority.

Netanyahu was asked by president Reuven Rivlin to try to form a government but his failure to do so saw a coalition of eight parties form a unity government under Prime Minister Naftali Bennett of Yamina and alternate Prime Minister Yair Lapid of Yesh Atid. However the coalition only had a single seat majority and the resignation of several members made the government unworkable.

Netanyahu's Likud party leads the opinion polls but at the time of going to press no group appeared to have a majority, suggesting yet more turmoil ahead. ✖

THE LATEST FROM OUR CAMPAIGNS

INDEX ON CENSORSHIP works on a number of active campaigns around the world. Find out more at indexoncensorship.org

Lukashenka's prisoners

Our letters from Lukashenka's prisoners campaign, where we publish correspondence from those jailed by the Belarusian regime, has now marked its first anniversary. Ala Sivets, an activist who works for Politzek.me, a project supporting political prisoners in Belarus, has asked why the letters are often full of encouragement and cheerful in tone.

"While human rights defenders and activists speak up about severe detention conditions and beatings, psychological pressure and denial of medical assistance, the picture from the prisoners' letters seems to be rather peaceful. Their imprisonment often looks like a retreat: they write about reading books and enjoying the fresh air during walks. The sharp contrast between the detention and what they write about may be confusing at first glance," she writes.
Read the full story at
tinyurl.com/Index513letters

FoI challenge in Malta

Index has joined with a number of free expression, press freedom and journalists' organisations to express support for The Shift News as it faces an all-out legal battle against 40 freedom of information (FOI) lawsuits brought by 40 government entities in Malta. These appeal lawsuits pose a serious threat to the country's already worrying freedom of information and press freedom climate. We call for these cases to be immediately dropped and for the government of Malta to fully comply

with its FOI obligations going forward.

The requests relate to a Shift News investigation into relations between Media Today co-owner Saviour Balzan and government entities in the country.
Read the full story at
tinyurl.com/Index513Malta

Index files alert after Sinn Féin MLA legal action

Index is concerned at the lawsuits that have been filed against journalist Malachi O'Doherty and columnist Ruth Dudley Edwards. Both are being sued individually by Sinn Féin politician Gerry Kelly MLA, who is claiming aggravated damages for comments they each made in relation to Kelly's role in 1983 Maze Prison escape.

"Everyone has the right to defend their good name but as elected representatives, politicians have a duty to display a greater degree of restraint when it comes to taking to legal action against journalists. This is especially true when the contested statements are related to matters of public interest," said Jessica Ní Mhainín, policy and campaigns manager at Index.
Read the full story at
tinyurl.com/Index513COE

Anti-SLAPP Coalition welcomes UK government's action

The co-chairs of the UK Anti-SLAPP Coalition have welcomed the announcement that the government intends to introduce a package of legislative measures aimed at putting an end to strategic lawsuits against public participation (SLAPPs) in the UK.

Noting that many of the UK Anti-SLAPP Coalition's recommendations are reflected in the proposals, the co-chairs commend the government for clearly stating its intention to introduce primary legislation to address this issue.
Read the full story at
tinyurl.com/Index513Slapps

The Index

PEOPLE WATCH

GUILHERME OSINSKI highlights the stories of human rights defenders under attack

Tharindu Uduwaragedara

SRI LANKA

Tharindu Uduwaragedara, a journalist from Sri Lanka, uses social media to cover human rights abuses. Uduwaragedara has been harassed for his work and subject to surveillance by security and intelligence officers.

At the end of June, Criminal Investigation Department officers headed to his mother's home to request Uduwaragedara's presence for an inquiry in Colombo. The explanation given was that this was happening due to the content shared on his YouTube channel, where Uduwaragedara frequently condemns the policies adopted by Sri Lanka's government.

Bolot Temirov

KYRGYZSTAN

Human rights defender Bolot Temirov has recently become one of the main targets of Kyrgyzstan's government. A few months ago, he was stripped of his Kyrgyz citizenship after his passport suddenly appeared as invalid in the database of the National Registration Agency.

Temirov reports on corruption. Before losing his passport, Temirov was accused of forgery of documents, illegal crossing of state borders and drug-related crime in what looks like a concerted campaign by authorities to silence him. If he is convicted, he could face up to 15 years in jail.

Maryam Karimbeigi

IRAN

Since 2009, human rights defender Maryam Karimbeigi has been striving to bring justice for the families of those murdered in peaceful protests in Iran. She began this journey when her brother, at the age of 26, was killed by Iranian police in 2009.

Karimbeigi defends the rights of political prisoners and campaigns against solitary confinement. On 14 June, she was sent to the notorious Evin Prison in Tehran.

In August, Karimbeigi was sentenced to three years and seven months. She was also fined and sentenced to 74 lashes as she had alcoholic drinks at her home.

Justyna Wydrzyńska

POLAND

Justyna Wydrzyńska is part of a group called the Abortion Dream Team, founded in 2016 with the purpose of supporting women looking for abortions. She's also behind Women on the Net, the first online forum in Poland to support those in search of abortions, contraception or sex education. In April, she was accused of "helping in the performance of an abortion", based on Article 152.2 of the Polish Penal Code, along with the "possession of unauthorised drugs". Her hearing will happen in October. If found guilty she'll be sentenced to three years in prison.

Ink spot

THIS CARTOON BY Palestinian-Jordanian artist Emad Hajjaj, well known in the Middle East for his cartoons featuring Abu Mahjoob – a character representing the Jordanian man in the street - was inspired by the 12 August attack on author Salman Rushdie as he prepared to give a talk at the Chautauqua Institution in New York State in the USA.

In August 2020, Hajjaj was arrested in Jordan under the country's cybercrime law for publishing a caricature criticising the Israel–United Arab Emirates peace agreement, showing the crown prince of Abu Dhabi holding a white peace dove on which is painted the Israeli flag.

Hajjaj has won the Dubai Press Award twice for best Arab cartoons and is considered one of the 500 most influential figures in the Arabic world, according to Arabian Business Magazine.

YOUR MESSAGES OF SUPPORT FOR SALMAN RUSHDIE

Following the brutal attack on Salman Rushdie in August, Index invited people to send him messages that we will share with him

ON 12 AUGUST 2022, Salman Rushdie, the author of the book The Satanic Verses, was attacked as he prepared to give a lecture at the Chautauqua Institution, an arts and education centre in New York State. He was stabbed in the neck, face and abdomen and, at the time of going to press, remained in a critical condition in hospital. His family issued a statement saying that despite his "life-changing injuries" being severe, "his usual feisty and defiant sense of humour remains intact".

Index has collaborated with Salman for decades now and fully support his right to freedom of expression, as we do for other authors and artists. Supporting those who are silenced, threatened and attacked is at the heart of Index's 50-year-long history. Index condemns this cowardly attack on the author.

INDEX CEO RUTH SMEETH said, "We are still in shock after the brutal attack on Salman Rushdie last week. While we are relieved to hear he survived, we know the path to recovery will be long and our thoughts go out to him and his family. We consider Salman part of the Index community. We were instrumental in the campaign against the fatwa and Salman has in turn written regularly for our magazine. He is a fierce defender of free expression and his writing, which is beloved by so many, is a testament to the power of words themselves."

She added, "The violence committed against him is an awful reminder that

the fight for freedom of expression continues and we are as committed as ever to campaigning for a world in which acts such as these never happen."

People from around the world are sharing their messages of support for the writer on our site – to be passed onto him.

A C GRAYLING wrote, "Censorship is unacceptable at the best of times, but censorship by bullying, threats, physical violence and murder is an abomination. It is the resort of those who are insecure and intellectually immature."

He added, "The attack on Salman Rushdie is an unforgivable example of what, if not resisted everywhere and always, would radically impoverish the world by silencing its art, thought and literature. The closed-minded seek not only to impose censorship but to frighten those who think differently from

them into self-censorship. They must be resisted. Rushdie is on the front lines of this struggle: we owe him our gratitude and unequivocal support."

MIRANDA MILLER in London said, "It seems that the fatwa against you has now been extended to allow all writers to be bullied, online and offline, by anyone who wants to be offended. I was particularly shocked to discover that the man who tried to murder you had only read two pages of your work. As a novelist, I feel it's our imaginations that are under attack."

DAVE BEAVERS, from Texas, wrote: "The attack on Rushdie is reprehensible and inexcusable, and his assailant needs to be held accountable to the fullest extent of the law and we have to be sure to send a message that these kinds of attacks on the very nature of free speech and expression will not and cannot be tolerated in any capacity."

He added, "We have to acknowledge that the very fatwa issued by the former Ayatollah Khomeini of Iran (the same responsible for holding the reins of the 1979 Islamic Revolution and the kidnapping and torture of American diplomats and civilians for over 400 days in Tehran at the end of the 1970s) is at the very HEART of this attack on Rushdie, decades after it was issued."

You can share your own messages with us at tinyurl.com/Index513Rushdie

The Index

TECH WATCH: INTERNET SHUTDOWNS

MARK FRARY on the rise of autocracies taking their online censorship to extremes

THE POWER OF the internet to give a voice to dissidents and to thwart censorship has made it a growing target for authoritarian governments, who sometimes opt to shut it down entirely.

A recent survey by VPN provider Surfshark found that internet shutdowns by governments across the world affected 1.89 billion citizens globally in the first half of 2022, a 22% increase on the second half of 2021. These included 66 state-mandated internet blackouts in six countries and territories: Burkina Faso, India, Jammu and Kashmir, Kazakhstan, Pakistan and Sudan.

Since then, Africa has become a continued focus for shutdowns.

On 10 August, the KeepItOn coalition reported that the authorities in Sierra Leone had instigated a two-hour internet shutdown as anti-government protests erupted in the capital Freetown, in response to the rising cost of living. This escalated quickly into violence, with reports of an unspecified number of deaths including police.

"This outrageous trend of governments flipping the kill switch in times of protests is increasingly alarming and cannot be allowed to become the new norm," said Felicia Anthonio, #KeepItOn campaign manager at Access Now.

"Authorities in Sierra Leone must be held accountable for shutting down the internet in order to quell the ongoing protests in the country rather than trying to pass it off as suspiciously timed 'maintenance' activities," Anthonio added.

The following day, the coalition said that journalists in Somaliland had reported an internet shutdown starting at 6am as protesters from the opposition and general public gathered in various locations, including Hargeisa and Burao. During the protests, the Woqooyi Galbeed region suffered a complete loss of internet traffic. The internet was restored by 4pm. The purpose of the shutdown was thought to be to avoid news of a violent response from government forces to the protests.

World In Focus: Nicaragua

Under the long-ruling President Daniel Ortega Nicaragua's rights landscape continues to deteriorate

1 Managuá
Yubrank Suazo, leader of the opposition to President Daniel Ortega in Nicaragua, was convicted in July and sentenced to 10 years behind bars due to 2018 protests against the ruling government.

Suazo was given five years for conspiracy and being a threat to national integrity and security, and a further five years for sharing and publishing fake news. In Nicaragua, it has become normal that trials of opposition leaders take place without the media present. The only person allowed at the trial was Maynor Curtis, his defence lawyer, who has vowed to appeal the conviction.

The Nicaraguan Center for Human Rights classified Suazo's verdict as a "judicial farce" and an unfair sentence.

2 Border with Costa Rica
The government of Nicaragua has recently expelled from its territory a group of nuns from the order founded by Mother Teresa. The nuns have been in Nicaragua since 1988 working for the poorest in the country, running a nursery, a home for abandoned and abused girls and a care home.

The official explanation for their expulsion by the authorities was that their group failed to meet their obligations to declare the origin of its funds. The same excuse regarding funding has been used to shut down more than 200 non-governmental organisations since 2018.

After a decision of Nicaragua's parliament to dismantle the legal status of the nuns, they were taken to the border with Costa Rica by the local police, where they were forced to cross on foot. The Catholic Church has criticised human rights abuses in the country, which has led to Ortega claiming that the Catholic clergy are "coup mongers" and "devils in cassocks".

3 El Chipote prison
In August 2021, Juan Lorenzo Holmann, general manager of the oldest daily newspaper in Nicaragua, La Prensa, was arrested on accusations of money laundering, although most believe his conviction is due to his opposition to Ortega. Holmann has been handed a nine-year sentence at El Chipote prison, near Montelimar beach on the Pacific coast of Nicaragua. The prison has one main purpose: to house political prisoners

The coalition has registered nearly 1,000 shutdowns in the past six years, with governments in Africa and Asia the biggest culprits.

A recent report by the UN Human Rights Council noted that shutdowns are powerful markers of deteriorating human rights situations. "Over the past decade, they have tended to occur in particular contexts, including during periods of conflict or heightened political tensions, such as the periods surrounding elections or during large-scale protests," it said and noted that almost half of the shutdowns recorded between 2016 and 2021 were carried out in the context of protests and political crisis.

The Council added, "While internet shutdowns deeply affect many human rights, they most immediately affect freedom of expression and access to information."

It has called on governments to establish "a collaborative mechanism for the systematic collection of information on mandated disruptions in which States, civil society and companies all contribute could make an enormous difference. This could include, for example, work to establish a comprehensive and publicly accessible database of orders to limit access to the internet or digital communications platforms, their underlying reasons and their scope." ✖

and opponents of Ortega's dictatorship.

Since Holmann's imprisonment, La Prensa has been forced to close its headquarters following a judicial decision, as well as the printworks responsible for printing their pages. The newspaper has moved to online only.

In July 2022, Holmann's mother, Ana Chamorro, revealed that she still hasn't lost faith and hopes to see her son again. Holmann has been getting weaker and is constantly ill.

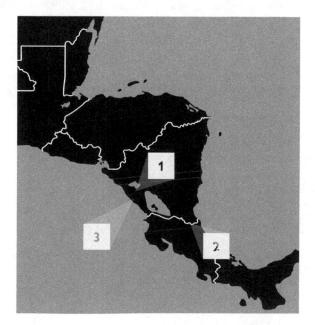

Free speech in numbers

34

Number of years prison sentence handed down to Salma al-Shehab for tweeting her support of prisoners of conscience in Saudi Arabia even though she was not in the country at the time

115

Number of books in the Collier County School District in Florida that bear labels warning readers that they include LGBTQ+ characters, sexual content and other material that might offend sensibilities

50.5%

Share of vote for William Ruto of the Kenya Kwanza Alliance in Kenya's disrupted presidential election in August

25

Kilograms of weight lost by Bahraini activist Dr Abduljalil al-Singace during a hunger strike that has lasted more than a year without solid food

232

The official number of deaths reported by the Kazakh government in June after anti-government protests in January

The Index

MY TRUTH SHOULD NOT BE BANNED

MY INSPIRATION

The bestselling US author **GEORGE M. JOHNSON** also holds the title of one of the US's most banned writers. Here they talk about keeping going

NSPIRATION COMES IN many forms. When people ask me "what is your inspiration" it is likely different based on the day and time and state of mind that I am in at the time. I've been inspired by people in life like my grandmother "Nanny", high school students I've met, to something as simple as a ladybug on the wall. That's the beautiful thing about inspiration though. It happens when you least expect it, but it always seems to come at the time you most need it.

When I wrote my debut memoir All Boys Aren't Blue, it was inspired by the death of a young queer teen. Simultaneously, it was inspired by the younger versions of me that I thought had died, but were very much alive in me waiting for their chance to speak. So the stories in that book weren't really from the 33-year-old me writing it. It was the 5-year-old me who knew he was different, but didn't know how to say it. And the 10-year-old me, and 15-year-old me, and even 20-year-old me who finally had those words to tell their truth. So that's what I did.

Unfortunately, I didn't know that me telling my truth would cause so many to be inspired to ban it. Inspire so much hatred that it be removed from the teens who need it most. But then two things happened. Their hatred inspired me to write even more stories, and be even more vocal about the story of the Black queer experience in the USA. And I watched the youth be inspired to say their truth. Find agency to fight for their rights to the materials and in many cases win and get the books back in their schools.

The youth keep me going. When I get messages and emails from teens and young adults across the country and the world about how my words are not only

ABOVE: The author George M. Johnson, whose memoir All Boys Aren't Blue was named the third most banned book in 2021 in the USA

helping them understand themselves but helping them heal it inspires me to keep doing the work. I once used to be that teen who had no resources about the struggles of my identity and sexuality. About the struggles of racism I was feeling when I was in high school. It is because of that I will continue to use the words to ensure that the future generations never have to feel the way I felt. May they too be inspired to tell their stories. ✖

George M. Johnson is the bestselling author of All Boys Aren't Blue

---

Free expression in peril in the Middle East and North Africa

Khalid Ibrahim, executive director of the Gulf Centre for Human Rights, writes about his organisation's recent campaigns

Free expression in the MENA region is under ongoing attack. Governments are using several means to imprison activists, including politicised judiciaries, terrorism and cybercrime laws as well as campaigns against them in state media.

In Saudi Arabia, Yemeni journalist Ali Mohsen Ahmed Abu Lahoum is still awaiting the decision on a request for reconsideration against the Court of Appeal's verdict upholding a 15-year prison sentence for his peaceful online activities. His family was recently prevented from visiting him in prison.

In the UAE, the authorities have again refused to release 40 prisoners of conscience despite the expiration of their sentences. Many are part of a group known collectively as the UAE94, who were arrested in 2012 and sentenced during an unfair trial for their pro-democracy activities.

In Iraq, public freedoms are at risk amid a political crisis in the country. Human rights defenders are constantly exposed to attacks and assassinations.

In Egypt, large numbers of human rights defenders are in prison. Some rights organisations have closed their doors due to repression, including one of the oldest in the region, the Arabic Network for Human Rights Information.

FEATURES

"Months before a museum director's contract runs out, the Ministry appoints a politically favoured successor - one with neither a reputation as cultural manager, artist or art theoretician"

MARTHA OTWINOWSKI | PERFECTING THE ART OF OPPRESSION, P.17

An unholy war on speech

Blasphemy charges are on the rise in Pakistan — and they often come with a death sentence. **SARAH MYERS** reports

THERE WAS NO light when I first saw Salma Tanveer's family. Her husband, Tanveer Ahmed, was using a smartphone to talk to translator and activist M Aman Ullah and me via Zoom. Where they were there were no windows, dusty concrete, a few dim light bulbs, and what seemed like people in desperate need of help.

Salma is a 50-year-old mother-of-two. In September 2021, she was sentenced to death by hanging for blasphemy.

She was first registered in a blasphemy case by police in 2013 for violating the Pakistan Penal Code, where she was found to be distributing material that claimed that she was the Holy Prophet.

"We were frequently visited by local clerics to give religious teachings to the children," explained her husband. "Salma frequently took notes and wrote down the speeches the clerics would give to the children."

One day, as Salma was writing the notes, the local clerics got hold of them to review what she had written. When

LEFT: A man reads the Koran in Karachi, Pakistan. The country's population is deeply religious and has been persecuting those who challenge Islamic teachings in recent years

the report was filed. But, despite the declaration, she has not been given treatment while in prison.

Her husband and Ullah have attempted to free her several times, including presenting her to the medical board where she had been declared a patient with schizoaffective disorder again. However, a doctor declared (in his opinion) that she was "70% fine and 30% not fine".

Salma is currently awaiting her sentence to be carried out.

"I am helpless," said Ahmed. "Five years ago, during the arrest, I had an accident where I broke one leg. I didn't get medical treatment at the time. I was pursuing the case against my wife when militants approached me and told me that if I were to continue to pursue this case they would break my other leg. I continued, and they broke my other leg.

"My daughter tried to commit suicide. She now lives with burns."

He walks over to the other side of the room to show me where his daughter lies on the bed. He lifts blankets and pulls at her clothes, where I see nothing but bandages covering her torso to her legs.

She needs to have "two or three" operations and her treatment costs him about $30 a day. The surgery for both of his legs will cost thousands of dollars.

"If I don't operate on my leg, one is about to give out. It's numb. I can't feel it anymore," he said.

Increased religious extremism started when the militant group known as the Tehrik-i-Taliban Pakistan (TTP) – the

Pakistani Taliban – was formed in 2007.

The Carnegie Endowment for International Peace states that the TTP is a Sunni Muslim group and its goals include establishing an Islamic political system based on its interpretation of sharia. Essentially, it would like to overthrow the government and replace it with a strict interpretation of Sharia.

The influence of religious extremist groups has spread across the country, with militant organisations forming in the more conservative cities.

And the threat of death by hanging as a result of a blasphemy charge is not unique to Salma Tanveer. A family of five – now three – were fighting these very groups by attempting to practise a more liberal form of Islam. Sehar, 28, Azad, 25, and Azan, 23, were three siblings living in Lahore, a city of approximately 15 million people.

"It is a very vibrant city," said Sehar, who added that it is safer in their current location than the countryside. But their lives changed after the alleged murder of their parents as a backlash to their liberal religious and political views.

"In 2018, we were living in an area where we were one of the few families receiving an education. I was getting my education and I was one of the few liberals in the area as an educated woman," explained Sehar. "People became jealous and started harassing me and started trying to stop me from getting an education. I do practise Islam as I am a believer of the religion, but I practise in a modern way."

This modern way included freedoms not traditionally given to women, such as the freedom to pursue an education and a career. The local community did not like the way Sehar was practising, so they targeted her family. →

they saw them, they filed a report under the penal code to the local police station under clauses A, B and C – the written law that stated one cannot commit blasphemy and can be punished by death. In those notes, Salma had written that she was the true apostle. The penal code states that Mohammed is the one and only true apostle.

"But when the case was registered, they fabricated the story," said Ahmed. "The photocopy of the notes had been changed and edited. They told the authorities that she wasn't mentally fit."

Salma had been diagnosed with schizoaffective disorder at the time

People became jealous and started harassing me and started trying to stop me from getting an education

→ "In Pakistan, there is a system where people send each other food, like sweet rice. Mother and father were home alone one day, and my mother ate the sweet rice that was delivered to her doorstep," she said.

After she ate the rice, Sehar's mother began developing breathing problems.

"I came to the house and took her to the hospital. The doctor said that she consumed something that attacked her lungs."

When the siblings tried to file an application to investigate the details of their mother's death, the neighbours and local clerics threatened them and said that if they filed one, the locals and the imam would file a blasphemy charge against the family.

The family obliged, not wanting to get in trouble. After their mother died, they went back to their normal routine, their jobs and universities. Then, one day when they returned home, they found their father on the floor of the house, dead.

Sehar thought someone had killed him by strangling him. The siblings wanted an investigation, but the clerics again threatened them with a blasphemy charge. "They said they would kill us if we did not leave our home and move away," said Sehar.

Her brother was followed and attacked, so the family sent him to Dubai – but he had to return because he only had a tourist visa. All three are currently unable to move freely or live openly, staying in a safe house organised and supported by Ullah.

"In Pakistan, clerics are the religious leaders. They influence people. They have big networks in Pakistan and, because of the fear, the siblings are reluctant to go outside during the

ABOVE: (left) Salma Tanveer, pictured with her children, and (right) Salma's husband also with the children. Salma is currently in prison having been charged with blasphemy

day," said Ullah. In 2012, Pakistan had 27 blasphemy cases ongoing, which frequently targeted religious minorities. In 2020, it registered 199 blasphemy cases taken to higher courts, often with little or no evidence.

In 2012, Ullah became involved with the rising number of cases. He first came into contact with a woman called Walaiha, who was 21 and imprisoned on a blasphemy charge. He hired lawyers and tried to find media and journalists to write about the case and help them get her to safety. He was successful in getting her out of prison but, when she was freed, Ullah received death threats as a result of his work. The pair married and Ullah fled to the Maldives, then to Sri Lanka, then to Dubai. They split up eight months later and he returned to Pakistan.

After his success in helping Walaiha, many more blasphemy victims approached him. He was involved with the high-profile case of Asia Bibi, a Roman Catholic from a village near Lahore, who was accused by Muslim villagers of insulting the Prophet in a row over a cup of water in June 2009. It

resulted in her spending eight years on death row before her release in 2018.

As many news organisations wrote, the country was shut down by protests based on the decision. Ullah's house was attacked, and his sister's wrist was broken. He fled the country with his mother and sisters in 2018, found Australian politicians who helped him, and then settled in Australia.

"I had to give up everything. I started a new life," he said.

Now he is helping Salma and her family and these three siblings, among others, and wants to start a non-profit organisation to raise awareness of religious blasphemy.

"I want to devote my life to the betterment of the people of my country," he said. "I have to fight. I need the support of Western leaders – people who are powerful. I want to spread education. To raise money.

"While I'm still trying to integrate into a new society, I'm still helping people in Pakistan because they believe I can help them."

In the meantime, Salma remains in jail, a death sentence over her head for something that should never be considered a crime. ✖

Sarah Myers is a writer living in New York City, USA

51(03):14/16|DOI:10.1177/03064220221126386

Their lives changed after the alleged murder of their parents as a backlash to their liberal religious and political views

CREDIT: Tanveer Ahmed

Perfecting the art of oppression

After just a few years running, Warsaw's Biennale says goodbye amid a wider crackdown on the creative industries in Poland. **MARTHA OTWINOWSKI** speaks to the people most affected

CREDIT: Monika Szolarska

THIS SUMMER, THE second edition of the Warsaw Biennale "Seeing Stones: Spaces Beyond the Valley" drew to a close – not just for the next two years, but for good; a victim of politics.

At the intersection of research and contemporary art, it brought together 50 international practitioners who interrogated the connections between global power structures, the digital sphere and infrastructure.

But the end of this exhibition cycle has not see the routine shift into the following curation phase that would lead to the next Biennale show two years from now – instead it marked the Warsaw Biennale's ceasing to exist as

ABOVE & P.20: A choir takes to the streets, co-organised by the Museum of Jewish Poles. There used to be a video recording of this event, which has since been used by PiS-party affiliates out of context as evidence of the Biennale's supposedly rogue activities

an institution. Staff members have been clearing out the offices for months, →

→ while the space has been turned into a makeshift refugee reception centre until the contract runs out.

What started out as an initiative by the city of Warsaw to support contemporary art in 2017 was reversed under the same party only a few years later - the neoliberal Civic Platform (PO). The reason is national politics, specifically a scandalisation of the first edition of the Warsaw Biennale in 2019.

It involved the mayor of Warsaw, Rafał Trzaskowski from the Civic Platform, who ran against the incumbent Andrzej Duda from the far-right Law and Justice (PiS) party as presidential candidate in 2020.

After narrowly losing the election, Trzaskowski is allegedly preparing himself for a potential second run. One thing is clear: he cannot use any bad press.

Any press is not good press

Bad press is what the Warsaw Biennale ended up costing Trzaskowski. Only weeks before the 2020 election, the national broadcaster TVP ran a piece titled: "3.6 million PLN [Polish Zloty] from Warsaw authorities for cultural institution training anarchists in 'urban tactics'", underscoring the agitated

> The removal of the politically uncomfortable Warsaw Biennale is exceptional

ABOVE & OPPOSITE: Images from this year's Biennale taken from an exhibition called Who has access?

tone of the piece with an image that - according to reverse image search - was taken at an unrelated event. While nominally a public service station, TVP has been under political influence by the Law and Justice party since 2015.

MPs of the PiS party subsequently questioned PO in Warsaw town hall on why "Trzaskowski was breeding his rainbow militias" in central Warsaw. Even after PiS won the presidential vote, the right-wing extremist group March for Independence brought a case against Trzaskowski to the National Public Prosecutor's Office accusing him of misconduct, making it clear the far right was not going to drop the topic.

CREDIT: Bartosz Górka / Biennale Warszawa

How come the far right scandalised the Warsaw Biennale as "an element of the 'communist international' " seeking to "overthrow by force prevailing systems"? In its first edition in 2019, the Warsaw Biennale ran under the title: "Let's Organize Our Future!" As curator for international programmes, Anna Galas-Kosil told Index the Biennale's focus stemmed from an observation that Polish politics was preoccupied with the opposite: "Given that the past was such a prominent topic in the political discourse, we wanted to facilitate a broader public debate on ways to imagine the future and discuss contemporary issues that we felt were important but under-served in the Polish public discourse."

As such, within one of its four core themes, Warsaw Biennale focused on democratic grassroot activities, bringing together dozens of Polish initiatives working across migrants' rights, women's rights, queer rights and environmentalism. A small number of events took place under what was termed the 'School of Anti-Capitalism'. Its objective, as stated on Warsaw Biennale's website, was to engage with ideas about "problems of rapidly growing economic inequalities and toxic individualism". The programme of the school reads as a critical theory-driven forum for exchanging ideas. For example, it includes a lecture by academic Simon Springer on his conception of capitalism as violent in its neoliberalisation processes.

Ironically, PiS itself successfully won a majority against the Civic Platform in 2015 precisely on an anti-neoliberal agenda. The Law and Justice-affiliated organisations and media, however, conceived of the Warsaw Biennale as a bootcamp for extremists.

The Civic Platform did not step in to defend the Warsaw Biennale, quite the contrary. In late 2020, local authorities informed the curators they wished to "shift the focus of the Biennale". In fact, behind this shift lay its scrapping and the rebuilding of a new organisation, specifically: The Warsaw Observatory of Culture. While the Biennale curators were invited to submit a proposal of their own for a competition held in early 2021, it was clear there was no way forward for the Biennale and the objectives it was built to pursue. Galas-Kosil told Index: "At the same time, the question remained as to the need of an observatory of the cultural sector on a local scale".

Tip of the cultural iceberg

The removal of the politically uncomfortable Warsaw Biennale is exceptional - given that it took place under the auspices of the ostensibly progressive, liberal Civic Platform in Warsaw.

However it fits into a wider trend that has affected almost all significant Warsaw cultural institutions, most of which are subordinate to the National Ministry for Culture and National Heritage: one by one, they are coming under political influence by the Law and Justice party. When it came to power in 2015, PiS initially focused on aligning other public institutions with its politico-ideological agenda, most prominently the media and the judicial system. Years later, its formerly branded 'good changes' have taken hold of almost all cultural institutions.

In most cases, the Ministry for Culture and National Heritage followed a specific blueprint. Months before a museum director's contract runs out, the Ministry appoints a politically favoured successor - one with neither a reputation as cultural manager, artist or art theoretician. And there is nothing illegal about this. Appointing new directors is within its remit, even though many in the cultural sector have been advocating a merit-based public call for applications.

This year, two crucial institutions came under PiS influence in this way: The National Contemporary Museum (Zacheta) in Warsaw as well as the Museum of Art (MS) in Łódź. Meanwhile, at the Centre of Contemporary Art Castle (Ujazdowski, CSW), the transformation has been underway for some time now. In late 2019, Piotr Bernatowicz was appointed its new director. Once in office, he cancelled several programmes curated by his predecessor Ludwisiak, claiming this was due to her inaccurate budgeting. Instead, the museum now had a twofold direction. First was exhibiting those who Bernatowicz viewed as previously not having been able to "exercise their creativity and freedom of speech", including highly controversial figures like Dan Park, known for defamatory depictions of ethnic minorities and use of Nazi symbols. A second, new raison d'être was providing an institutional framework to commemorate historic events to further a 'Polish sense of self'. For anniversary celebrations of a victory against the Red Army in 1920, for example, the CSW organised a 'Free World' open air concert, to which it invited the Hungarian far right band Hungarica. It ultimately felt compelled to retreat from this decision after even →

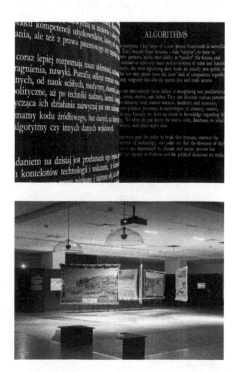

→ the national broadcaster TVP reported on the band's problematic affiliations.

Sneaking behind the scenes

Index exclusively spoke to Michał Matuszewski, who was cinema and film curator at Ujazdowski. During his 13 years at the institution, he witnessed three different directors.

Along with a small number of colleagues, Matuszewski decided to stay on and oppose the anticipated political influence. And Bernatowicz's taking up office in early 2020 started fairly inconspicuously. Unlike other PiS-installed directors before him - notably the controversial and noisy Miziołek at the National Museum - no one was let go. However, over the span of two years, Matuszewski said, Bernatowicz put in place a set of circumstances that practically forced Matuszewski out of his job.

Months into the new directorship, an inexperienced colleague was hired to work on a par with Matuszewski in a senior role. As daughter of Maciej Pawlicki, a film director known for his vocal PiS party line, she was trusted to

follow in his ideological footsteps. After only two years, she was promoted to being Matuszewski's supervisor, leaving him without any tasks of his own.

Matuszewski says: "It's extremely disheartening for me to have to leave and painfully witness the sneaking, hostile takeover of yet another cultural institution of the country. At this point, there are countless examples for the mind-boggling programme choices of CSW over the past 2.5 years, only one of which we could stop. But the way in which I have had to leave - I have had to grapple with this for months - I don't wish on anyone."

Matuszewski has been observing Bernatowicz installing inexperienced, loyal staff across all CSW departments and suspects this to be a strategy with the goal to frustrate employees opposing the PiS-agenda.

Is PiS willingly rendering Poland's art institutions irrelevant? Matuszewski says: "That's not their reasoning. Those behind this takeover argue this is an emancipation project for pluralism as, allegedly, right-wing art had been censored before. But the desired result

is that any perspective not aligned with the party stance should be eradicated with no trace left behind. The cultural sector is yet another battleground in ideological warfare."

Until recently, observers feared the Museum of Modern Art in Warsaw (MSN) would be next. However, it has escaped that fate for now. Unlike most Warsaw institutions, the MSN was not exclusively under the auspices of Poland's National Cultural Ministry, but also the city of Warsaw. This May, a Warsaw City Council vote transferred the MSN exclusively to Warsaw city, meaning less funding and an overall lower profile for the institution. Speaking under condition of anonymity, someone employed at a different art institution in Warsaw told Index that they viewed this move as an act of desperation: "They cut off their arm to save themselves."

The motivation behind this is that the Civic Platform has held a majority in Warsaw for many years. But this approach is not without risk. What if Law and Justice ever won a Warsaw election? And, the example of the Warsaw Biennale is evidence that PO is just as capable of removing cultural institutions which have become uncomfortable politically.

Co-curator Galas-Kosil told Index: "In the end, the case of the Biennale illustrates that both major parties are not too far apart in how they operate or in the role they attribute to contemporary art. Just like PiS taking over all these institutions, the PO has dismantled a contemporary art institution, just on the off chance it might cause them issues in the future. Many cities would dream of the type of intersectional discussion the Biennale provided, but this is not something that is politically desired." ✖

Martha Otwinowski is a Berlin-based journalist, who reports from Poland and Germany

51(03):17/20|DOI:10.1177/03064220221126389

Poland's redemption songs

As populism, authoritarian rule and war grip Eastern Europe,
MARTIN BRIGHT remembers a time when everything seemed possible

S I WALKED away from Gdansk railway station on 13 December 1989, I was greeted with a sight I will never forget. Shuffling through the bone-chilling snow were hundreds of young Poles, many of them with dreadlocks, heading to a reggae concert in the city's famous shipyard as if it was the most normal thing in the world. It was my first glimpse of the surreal youth culture of Iron Curtain Poland and its obsession with the rebel music of Jamaica.

The concert was being held to mark the anniversary of martial law, introduced in 1981 as an attempt to crush the Solidarity trade union movement that started in 1980. The military had failed; the tanks had left the streets. And Solidarity, which began with Polish shipyard workers, grew to inspire the revolutions that swept Eastern Europe at the end of the decade, ultimately leading to the fall of the Berlin Wall on 9 November 1989.

I watched those events on a battered TV in a shabby housing co-op (one step up from a squat) in Hackney, east London and realised I had to be there. I sold most of my possessions and bought a return ticket to Berlin. But then I heard about this crazy reggae peace concert in Gdansk, so I took a train to Poland. I still have the ticket and an →

BELOW: Linton Kwesi Johnson in Gdansk shipyard, Poland, in 1989

> They had not had a history of slavery but they understood what it was to suffer

LEFT: Marlene Johnson at the "Africa" reggae festival in Poland, 2009

→ old cassette (see insert). It shows the event was intended not just to celebrate Poland's fight for freedom but as an act of solidarity with the anti-apartheid movement in South Africa. Looking back, there was a naïve, global ambition to the event which suited the optimism of the times. If the Berlin Wall could fall, then anything was possible (and, sure enough, two months later Nelson Mandela was free, and apartheid was effectively over).

Speaking in Gdansk to the BBC at the time, the celebrated dub poet Linton Kwesi Johnson eloquently expressed the significance of the concert: "Solidarity's spirit of internationalism is great — that on the eighth anniversary of martial law they should be holding an anti-apartheid show. And I'm so pleased that so many Black musicians have been invited, because we too have a history of struggle and we too can identify with the oppressed people of Poland."

The first person I met in Gdansk was Miroslaw "Maken" Dzieciolowski, who helped me find my hotel while explaining his love of hardcore punk and reggae in a unique Polish patois picked up from the music he loved. He was the most

enthusiastic person I had ever met. Three decades on, speaking to Index from his home in Warsaw over Zoom, he still has the ear-to-ear grin I remember from Gdansk railway station. Now 54, he also has a magnificent set of greying dreadlocks as befits an elder statesman of Polish reggae. I asked him why he thought this particular music had such a hold on young Poles at the time.

"I think mostly because it was freedom music. It always carried a message of freedom," he said. Maken went on to make a life as a Polish reggae promoter, bringing major British and Jamaican musicians to Poland in the decades after the collapse of Communism. Was there also a spiritual side to it? "They were looking for some spiritual values, but in opposition to the Church. True values, true feelings, not

anything institutional. Nothing fake. People were looking for true music."

Brinsley Forde, star of the British reggae band Aswad, was the MC at the concert that night. He had travelled to Gdansk from Warsaw on a bus so cold that the blanket he was using as a pillow froze to the window. He'd been told about the concert by a friend at the BBC and travelled with the legendary producer and musician Denis Bovell, whose band was playing for Linton Kwesi Johnson. Forde was originally planning to watch from the audience and was only asked to host the event when he arrived in Poland. At the time he didn't realise the significance of reggae to the Polish people. Three decades on he has had time to think about it: "You have to understand they had been oppressed first by the German occupation, then the Russian occupation. They had not had a history of slavery but they understood what it was to suffer. It was a rebel music from the ghetto, standing up for the people."

The organisers of the concert were a combination of Solidarity trade union officials and local Polish reggae fans. These included Wlodzimierz Kleszcz, whose radio show helped introduce underground music, including reggae, to a Polish audience, and his brother Jurek.

Jurek now lives in the UK and spoke to Index from his home in Brighton. "In Poland, reggae came out of the punk scene and some off-the-beaten-track festivals, which took place even during the time of martial law. You

CREDIT: (festival) Leszek Kozlowski/Flickr; (cassette) Martin Bright

Maken remembers the dark days of state censorship when concert promoters had to get official stamps on a band's lyrics for a show to get the go-ahead

have to remember that officially you couldn't perform unless all the lyrics or your songs were approved by the censor. That was the reality in Poland." Like Forde, he believed the music represented rebellion: "It was a way for young people to express themselves in opposition to what was happening."

The concert itself was only made possible by the political earthquake in Poland which had brought Solidarity-backed candidates to power in legislative elections in the summer of 1989. It was, in part, a celebration of the role reggae had played in inspiring the spirit of resistance in those dark years. The line-up included big stars of the reggae scene at the time: Benjamin Zephaniah, Bob Andy and Twinkle Brothers, along with Kwesi Johnson, Bovell and Forde. But local acts also played: Gdansk reggae band Rocka's Delight and even a Polish jazz act called, appropriately, Young Power. Thanks to support Solidarity secured with the international trade union movement, there was also a group of South African singers and dancers, Bambaata's Children of Natal, who

It's not a result of any written regulations. But you know if you discuss some things in some manner, you are risking a lot

performed a tribute to Mandela.

The Gdansk event was the culmination of years of underground activity that began with a band who couldn't be there that night. Misty in Roots, a firm favourite of the cult British DJ John Peel, had shunned the conventions of the music business in favour of touring Africa, Eastern Europe and Russia in the early 1980s. In 1983 they played around 20 shows across Poland with the now legendary early Polish reggae act, Israel. "Shortly afterwards," Maken explained, "in every town they played, there were new Polish reggae bands. It was incredible. It caused the first and biggest movement of reggae in Poland with local bands — like hundreds."

There was even an official Communist release of the classic Misty in Roots album, Live at the Counter Eurovision '79. Little did the authorities realise that in promoting music they thought was anti-western and anti-colonial, they were encouraging rebellion against their own regime.

The artists involved that day back in December 1989 were deeply affected by the event. Linton Kwesi Johnson even wrote a poem, Mi Revalueshanery Fren, about the political discussions on that freezing bus from Warsaw to Gdansk. Norman Grant, the leader of Twinkle Brothers, took his creative engagement even further, collaborating with the Polish band Trebunie-Tutsi, fusing reggae with the traditional music of the Tatra Mountains. And Brinsley Forde took the ultimate step of moving to Poland, where he now runs a Caribbean restaurant Boomshakala in Krakow, with his Polish partner (who showed him her prized cassette of the Gdansk concert when they first met). Reggae still remains hugely popular in Poland, with

the Ostroda festival being one of the largest in Europe devoted to the genre. The Brinsley Forde Aswad Experience, in which the reggae star plays with local musicians, was one of the highlights of the festival last summer.

Maken, like Jurek, remembers the dark days of state censorship when concert promoters had to get official stamps on a band's lyrics for a show to get the go-ahead. He was also responsible for releasing a cassette of censored music in the 1980s.

But Maken recognises that all is not well with free expression in Poland today, particularly anything that challenges the socially conservative values of the governing Law and Justice Party. Maken still runs a radio show and knows he has to be careful. He told Index that it's sometimes harder now because it's unclear where the boundaries of free expression lie for broadcasters and musicians.

"At that time, there were some rules, and now, it's secret. I've witnessed it sometimes with my people on the radio. They are really afraid of touching some issues. But it's not a result of any written regulations. But you know if you discuss some things in some manner, you are risking a lot," he said.

For Maken, Brinsley and Jurek, the Gdansk Solidarity-anti-apartheid was a defining moment in their lives. The same is true for me. It's difficult to say exactly why it had such a profound effect on all of us. Maybe because it was one of those rare moments of undiluted optimism, where the good guys looked like they were winning. ✖

Martin Bright is editor-at-large at Index

51(03):21/23|DOI:10.1177/03064220221126394

ABOVE: An original cassette from the festival

Fighting back against vendetta politics

As its government cracks down on criticism, **HANAN ZAFFAR** and **HAMAAD HABIBULLAH** talk to India's journalists and activists about dwindling freedoms

UNTIL 2017 MOHAMMED Zubair was a telecoms engineer with a secure job in Bangalore – a city termed the "Silicon Valley" of India. Since then, he has transformed himself into the country's leading fact-checker: busting fake news, misinformation and propaganda often associated with – and pushed by – the ruling right-wing regime and its large base of supporters.

The transformation was driven by circumstances – a need to halt the exponential magnitude and penetration of the misinformation, often politically motivated, that sweeps India every day.

But confronting the people at the helm can land you in trouble, and Zubair ended up behind bars. It wasn't the first time he'd been arrested. He has been actively at odds with India's ruling Bharatiya Janata Party (BJP) due to his fact-checking work. His most recent clash with the authorities was on 27 June, when he was arrested for a tweet he posted four years ago of an image from a decades-old film.

He was accused of insulting a Hindu god after an anonymous Twitter user made a complaint.

Police charged Zubair in different states under sections of the country's penal code, including for "giving provocation with intent to cause riots" and "deliberate and malicious acts, intended to outrage religious feelings", and was released on bail three weeks after his arrest.

But in today's India, Zubair's arrest isn't an aberration – it is the norm. Dozens of other journalists and activists have been hounded by the Hindu nationalistic regime in India for criticising its policies and narratives.

"His work has had direct implications on the government, often becoming a source of embarrassment for them," Pratik Sinha, who co-founded fact-checking website Alt-News with Zubair, told Index.

"For the last few years, he has exposed the misinformation and hate speeches that the government and its supporters have indulged in. That's why he was put behind bars."

Before his arrest, Zubair had called attention to the derogatory remarks by a BJP spokesperson against the Prophet of Islam, which resulted in backlash from within and outside India. The ruling BJP is accused by its critics of furthering Islamophobia and targeting minorities, particularly marginalised Muslims.

Sinha said the country had been going through an undeclared emergency for some time, adding: "This government is crushing every opposing voice."

As well as Zubair, numerous journalists and activists have been targeted by the authorities for their criticism of the government. The Committee to Protect Journalists' 2021 prison census (a snapshot in time, rather than a summary of the year) found seven journalists were in prison in India on the

> ≡ **This government is crushing every opposing voice**

final day of the year. The organisation said this was the highest number of detained journalists in the country since 1992 and also reported that, in 2021, four journalists were killed there because of their work. Meanwhile, Reporters Without Borders (RSF) said that 10 journalists were in prison in India as of August 2022.

"These arrests are a clear indication that the constitutional values, freedom of speech and dissent are being targeted and attacked by the current government, which is indulging in vendetta politics," said Abhay Kumar, a journalist and political commentator based in New Delhi. "Anybody, be it a journalist, activist or a common citizen who is not speaking the language of the government, is now being targeted. We have a liberal and secular constitution, but the current majoritarian regime is targeting people – particularly those belonging to minority sections."

Quratulain Rehbar, a prominent freelance journalist from the conflict-torn Indian-administered Kashmir, who has also faced government intimidation several times for her critical coverage of its policies, believes the current environment of persecuting journalists who are not toeing the state's line has led to large-scale self-censorship.

"Government had already silenced the mainstream and local media which did not report on issues like human rights and minorities," she said. "Such issues were mostly reported by the freelance journalists, who are also being intimidated, beaten, summoned for questioning and even arrested. This is not less than an emergency when it comes to freedom of speech."

She recounted her many colleagues – such as Fahad Shah, Siddique Kappan

and Asif Sultan – who have been jailed by the authorities. Many of these journalists were arrested and charged under India's anti-terror laws including the Unlawful Activities (Prevention) Act, which allows authorities to jail them for months without any incriminating evidence.

"I now have to rethink a lot of times before doing any story," said Rehbar, who has also been the target of several co-ordinated attacks by online trolls. In one of the attacks she, along with dozens of other Muslim journalists and activists, was "auctioned" online on an app called Bulli Bai. "The situation for journalists and journalism is grim," she added.

In the latest RSF press freedom index, India has slipped to 150th place out of 180 – a slide of eight positions from last year. Over the years, the country has seen a consistent slip in its ranking, owing to the treatment of journalists, and specifically those who are critical of the government.

Critics of the government fear the worst is yet to come. Shabnam Hashmi, a veteran activist who often speaks up against Prime Minister Narendra Modi's regime, said she didn't find the government's actions surprising.

"We are living in a semi-fascist state," she said. "When you are living in such conditions then the biggest enemies are the people who speak and write.

"If you look at the history of any dictators, dictatorship or authoritarian regime, you will find that the attack comes on writers, poets, journalists, anybody who raises questions. So that is what is happening in our country."

She offers a bleak prophecy for India: "With this ideology and politics, we as a country seem to be doomed." ✖

*Hanan Zaffar is a journalist and a researcher at OP Jindal Global University in Sonipat, India and **Hamaad Habibullah** is a journalist and a media scholar at Jamia Millia Islamia University in New Delhi*

51(03):24/25|DOI:10.1177/03064220221126395

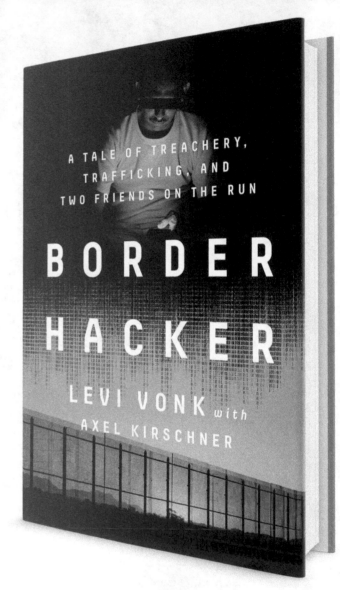
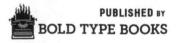

The mafia state that is putty in Putin's hands

Rumour has it that influential people in Bulgaria are being paid by the Kremlin to spread its lies. **MARK SEACOMBE** reports from Sofia

GIVE ME YOUR OLIGARCHS, YOUR DIRTY MONEY, YOUR OIL&GAS!

THE WEST

PUTIN

CHRISTO KOMAR

"FUCK PUTIN!" SHOUTS the message scrawled in red on litter bins near the monument to the Soviet army in the heart of the Bulgarian capital.

Millions of people nationwide agree with that response to the invasion of Ukraine – a neighbour across the Black Sea – although they might not necessarily put it so crudely.

This story is complicated because millions of others disagree after being inveigled into believing Russian President Vladimir Putin's big lies that his country is defending itself against Nato aggression and fighting to rid Ukraine of neo-Nazis and fascists.

While the shells mercilessly pound the Donbas region of eastern Ukraine, the Kremlin is bombarding Bulgaria with propaganda about what it calls

ABOVE & OVERLEAF: How cartoonist Christo Komarnitski sees Putin's war in the pages of the liberal weekly Sega

its "special military operation" and others see as an unjustified war. And Russia's assault on a traditional Slavic ally, hitherto its closest friend in the European Union, is working. About a quarter of the population of nearly seven million still support Putin, according to polls – although that is down from about a third before the killing began.

An already precarious society – widely labelled, like Putin's Russia, a "mafia state" because of its corruption – Bulgaria is now further divided. It is the kind of discord that a resentful Putin likes to sow among perceived foes, especially those

that, back in the USSR, were part of the communist family. The dictator Todor Zhivkov, ousted in 1989 shortly after the Berlin Wall fell, was the most slavishly loyal of east European leaders.

Today, the EU's poorest nation per capita is firmly in the Nato camp and the relationship between the two countries has dramatically deteriorated – economically, politically and diplomatically – since the war in Ukraine began in February.

In the summer, the poison from Moscow – on television, in the newspapers and on Facebook, the most popular social media network – is believed to have been a factor in the toppling of the fledgling reformist coalition government. It had come to power in December 2021 after mass demonstrations against the regime of Prime Minister Boyko Borissov, once Zhivkov's personal bodyguard. Bulgaria now faces its fourth parliamentary election in two years on 2 October.

When the war broke out – shortly after Borissov's defenestration – his successor, Kiril Petkov, took an anti-Putin, pro-Ukraine stance and gave refuge initially to about half a million people fleeing the bloodshed.

In turn, in April, Moscow cut off the gas supply to a nation dependent on it and launched cyberattacks on Bulgaria's state energy company. This was followed in June by Sofia's expulsion of 70 Russian diplomats, most of them for spying.

In the run-up to the expulsions, Petkov summoned Putin's combative ambassador, Eleonora Mitrofanova, after she described Bulgaria as the "bedpan" of the USA. In an interview with The New York Times, the prime minister said Mitrofanova was "acting not like a diplomat but a propaganda machine".

Amid this tumult, Teodora Peeva is depressed and angry. She is editor of Sega, a liberal and independent newspaper – a rare creature in Bulgaria – and a campaigner for press freedom in a country ranked second worst in →

It is the kind of discord that a resentful Putin likes to sow among perceived foes

→ the EU, after Greece, in the Reporters Without Borders World Press Freedom Index 2022. Bulgaria's media is described as "fragile and unstable".

Peeva, the paper's editor since 2005, is upset because "the government has done nothing to stop the flow of propaganda", she told Index.

In concert with the rest of the EU, Bulgaria had banned RT (formerly Russia Today), the international TV network funded by the Kremlin. "But what was the point when people can turn on the TV any time and hear pro-Russian views, in Bulgarian, from commentators and politicians?" she asked.

She said Trud, a brash tabloid daily, reprinted pro-Putin stories from Russian newspapers. One of these stories, from the tabloid Komsomolskaya Pravda, falsely claimed that the Ukrainian soldiers under siege for weeks in the Azovstal steel plant in Mariupol were Nazis. Trud said the report justified the invasion.

"That was terrible," said Peeva, "but they do it all the time."

She was in no doubt, she said, that the toxic atmosphere generated by disinformation about Ukraine had helped to bring down the government,

which was felled when it lost a vote of confidence.

So what did she make of the claim by Lena Borislavova, the outgoing prime minister's spokesperson and head of the political cabinet, that, according to the Bulgarian secret services, the Kremlin was paying Bulgarian politicians, journalists and other prominent people to spread its propaganda?

Borislavova had told a TV network that there was evidence that the influential people, whom she did not name, were being paid 4,000 leva (about $2,114) a month.

"Well, my reaction is that 4,000 leva isn't very much!" said Peeva, laughing derisively. "I know people – politicians – who boast of being paid by the Russians. And they wouldn't get out of bed for 4,000 leva a month; 4,000 a minute, maybe."

Most of the people speaking up for Putin in the media did not believe what they were saying. "They are just doing it for the money," she said – but in this case much more than 4,000 leva.

"The big problem in Bulgaria is media freedom, or the lack of it," said Peeva, whose paper began as a daily in 1997 but, in order to survive, was forced to turn weekly just before the pandemic began. "Even those politicians who want to reform the system – to end corruption – don't understand this. They don't like criticism."

And because trust in the independence of the mainstream media was so low among the public – down to about 10%, according to polls – people were forced to go online for information, she said.

About 70% of Bulgarians get their news from social media, according to the Digital News Report 2021 by the Reuters Institute at Oxford University.

While the trolls generated by the

Kremlin's vast propaganda machine are anonymous, Bulgaria's pro-Russian politicians are visible, audible and unapologetic. Peeva described the ultra-nationalist party Revival and the Bulgarian Socialist Party – key parts of the collapsed coalition – as "the public faces of Russian propaganda in Bulgaria today".

Revival, which won almost 5% of parliamentary seats last December, is led by Kostadin Kostadinov, who was banned from entering Ukraine at the start of the war, suspected of being a Russian agent. He has a lively following of 270,000 on Facebook and has organised "peace" demonstrations in Sofia in support of Putin. The Socialists, formed from the remnants of the old Communist Party, have their own TV network, Bulgarian Free Television, which broadcasts pro-Putin propaganda, according to Peeva.

You do not have to go far in Sofia to encounter those who have bought into

CREDIT: (all images) Christo Komarnitski

the Kremlin narrative.

"The world says Putin is the bad guy, but I think he is just defending his country from the Americans who wanted to occupy Ukraine," Yniki Ynikiev, aged 16, told Index. "Most people who say the Ukrainians are good people didn't study history. I think they are Nazis and fascists. Not all of them, of course."

Ynikiev, who was promoting Nescafé in the gardens of the National Palace of Culture, a brutalist concrete behemoth built in 1981 at the height of the Zhivkov regime, said his information came from the internet and TV.

But why does a bright young man like Ynikiev, and so many of his compatriots, believe the Russian version of the "truth"?

"Partly because they want to – and partly for historical reasons," the (outgoing) minister for e-government, Bozhidar Bozhanov, told Index. "For a long time – because of our ties – we have been taught history from an angle that favours Russia. So people are primed to accept things that glorify the Russian army, that say how great Putin is – and, therefore, how decadent the West is, how aggressive Nato is, how the EU is crumbling. As the old cliché goes, if you repeat the lies for long enough, they do not become true but people start suspecting that they may be true."

Speaking in his office at the ministry he set up at the beginning of 2022, Bozhanov said: "It is absolutely vital and healthy to have a debate about what is true and what is not true. But when a nation state – Russia – interferes in this debate, using all the techniques that they have mastered in the Cold War, and applies them to social media platforms, then things become complicated for

citizens trying to find their way out of the maze."

Asked whether Russian propaganda was a threat to democracy in Bulgaria, he said yes. And he was certain that the Kremlin would interfere in the campaign for the October election and try to influence its outcome using people in Sofia sympathetic to Putin.

One of the political leaders that the Russians will be backing is the controversial Socialist leader Korneliya Ninova, the deputy prime minister in the fallen coalition. Her party opposes Bulgarian arms sales to Ukraine and at one point she threatened to collapse the government over the issue.

An IT expert, Bozhanov aims to help Bulgarians to negotiate the maze of information and misinformation by trying to squeeze details out of Facebook about its workings via the new EU Digital Services act (approved by Strasbourg this summer). But he is

not holding his breath waiting for Mark Zuckerberg's colossus to reveal much about its key recommendation engine – what determines the newsfeed, what it shows and what it does not show. He described this as "a black hole".

The Act, the purpose of which was to outlaw "harmful" material on the web, was of little use against much of the Russian disinformation, he said. "The propaganda isn't, by definition, harmful content; it is not even always completely false – it may be 60% or 70% true in some cases. Just taking something out of context, putting a little touch on it to make it fit the narrative ... That's propaganda; that's how it works."

Not harmful per se, perhaps, but propaganda can hurt as well as distort. Imagine being among the 87,500 Ukrainian refugees – predominantly women and children – now settled on the Black Sea coast, nearly 400 kilometres east of Sofia. You switch on the TV or scroll through Facebook, only to be confronted with the lie that Putin's butchery is a just cause. ✖

Mark Seacombe is a freelance journalist

51(03):27/29|DOI:10.1177/03064220221126396

> You do not have to go far in Sofia to encounter those who have bought into the Kremlin narrative

Bodies of evidence

Journalism has taken a new turn, requiring skills that would be the envy of forensic investigators. **SARAH SANDS** spoke to its trailblazers

BELOW: Stabilised and 'motion tracked' video footage is projected back onto a model of London's Grenfell Tower, the scene of a devastating fire in 2017

CREDIT: Forensic Architecture

THE JOURNALISM THAT I practised over 40 years in newspapers and at the BBC was, at its best, a pursuit of truth.

Crucially, we did it in competition with other news organisations. Speed was all. When we covered big events, we might claim a stab at the first draft of history.

At the Evening Standard in the days of hot metal, a front-page scoop would last all day. As the sellers called out "Read all about it!" they could be confident that nobody already had.

The arrival of new techniques and the notion of "citizen journalism" was treated with scepticism by Fleet Street.

How would amateur observers know what they were looking at? Veracity and corroboration would go out the window, names would be spelled incorrectly, the pursuit of truth would end up in a maze. Who could we trust? Naturally, we were disinclined to discuss questions about our own objectivity.

And now here I am, 40 years after setting out as a local news reporter, in the cool, pale premises – part technology hub, part gallery, part laboratory – of Forensic Architecture, a multidisciplinary group based at Goldsmiths, University of London. I am witnessing the future of investigative journalism, using techniques so

advanced that I feel like a town crier.

Forensic architecture is alchemising data, images and sound from smartphones, CCTV, satellites, audio recordings, weather reports, government documents and anything else that might be relevant. It is bringing a new dimension to journalism.

To understand what is happening, we must first understand a little about Bellingcat – the investigative agency founded by Eliot Higgins, who started his journalistic enterprise blogging under the name of Brown Moses.

As he put it at the time: The Press is dying, long live the news. Generations of journalists learned to ask: who, what, why, where and when? The Bellingcat motto is identify, verify, amplify.

Higgins, perhaps the most influential journalist of our age, was not trained as a reporter. He was quick to understand the range of open-source material in a computer age, the testimony that emerged from mobile phones cross-checked with databases and free satellite maps, the expected lists of names and functions and roles. He realised that being in the thick of the action was not necessarily enlightening and offered only a snapshot of the truth. The new investigative journalism is multi-sourced and multi-layered, raising evidence to the standard of the international courts.

This is where forensic architecture offers a whole new level. Eyal Weizman is professor of spatial and visual cultures at Goldsmiths and heads the Centre for Research Architecture, the first of its kind in the world. He said: "Wars are fought first on the ground and public perception, then in the courts and history."

When we meet, I ask if I may tape the conversation and he gives a little smile. Tape! A particle of evidence. His department understands that journalism, if it is to achieve its noble function of truth-finding, is multi-disciplinary. His colleagues are architects, engineers, coders, film makers, legal experts.

The department used technology in 2020 to establish the facts of an inflammatory episode in Hebron, in the West Bank, when a former Israeli officer, Dean Issacharoff, confessed to assaulting a Palestinian. It was asked to produce a photorealistic 3D model of the event, re-creating the alley where the assault took place and walking witnesses through it with the aid of virtual reality goggles.

Weizman, born in Israel, remembers the architecture of occupation – "bridges, roads, walls".

This kind of reconstruction is an extraordinary tool for reliving memory. One of Weizman's colleagues shows me on his screen a 3D model of London's Grenfell Tower on the night it caught fire in the summer of 2017.

Conventional media would show a picture of the tower on fire and interview witnesses. Forensic Architecture walks you to the building from various angles and can accurately say how and where fire-filled debris would have fallen.

Weizman says: "We understood something very simple, which was that the architecture model that we were building was a very powerful way to synchronise and locate an incident. So you have an incident and a few seconds later – it takes people about five seconds to switch on their smartphones – there are different perspectives. People report different things, but through locating those video sources we can weave them into a story which is precise."

Traditional journalism in the field communicates drama and atmosphere but cannot give you a complete picture.

It was important for journalists headed for Kyiv in late February to record Russia's invasion. Audiences understood the severity of what was happening but, apart from news graphics, it was hard to follow the developments of battles or be clear about the numbers of casualties. Raw social media was little help.

Weizman says: "Very often we see material on social media but what they communicate is chaos – sometimes journalists use it smartly to communicate chaos almost like a roll: here is a place, jagged video, narrative voice – but it is not actually a piece of evidence."

In taking on state injustice,

investigative journalism needs to be of a standard fit for prosecution. Anyone who has seen the remarkable documentary Navalny, exploring the Russian opposition leader Alexey Navalny, can only admire this new era of journalism.

Bellingcat is now establishing an innovation lab in Berlin along with Forensic Architecture, Syrian Archive and the European Centre for Constitutional and Human Rights (ECCHR) – a non-governmental organisation that uses litigation to hold the guilty responsible.

The idea is a centre of excellence for open-source techniques: Bellingcat for the online investigations, the department of forensic architecture applying technological tools to visualising and expanding evidence, Syrian Archive preserving digital records and the ECCHR ensuring such material helps to enforce human rights.

The centre must pick and choose the cases it takes on. It is not going to become the Reuters news agency, but each time it does investigate, it innovates further. It is likely at some point to support investigations into war crimes committed in Ukraine, but it also sheds light on historical events, suggesting criminals can never be confident of escaping their past.

Researcher Imani Jacqueline Brown gives me a detailed account of a project to investigate genocide by Germany in Namibia in the early 20th century, subjecting collective memory and contemporaneous testimony to corroboration by locating ancestral homesteads and burial grounds.

In 1904, German colonial troops mistook a gathering of Ovaherero men as a mass mobilisation and mounted an attack in Okahandja, forcing the people from their ancestral homeland. The Ovaherero sought a peace treaty at Waterberg, but German troops blocked them, forcing them into arid land. Concentration camps were established across the country and there was an international trade in human skulls. While 80% of the Ovaherero →

The new investigative journalism is multi-sourced and multi-layered, raising evidence to the standard of the international courts

CREDIT: Forensic Architecture

→ were wiped out, descendants record ancestral memories.

Would it be possible to prove these colonial crimes? Phase one of the project is identifying partners within local communities and testing methodologies. Already they have identified scenes of conflict and, sure enough, German weapons have been excavated there. Phase two, next year, will map and model sites where atrocities are believed to have taken place, locating concentration camps that used forced labour. The researchers plan 3D scans of mass graves in the Namib desert. They will geo-locate archival photographs to prove the dispossession of communities.

Descendant families sit with an architectural researcher in front of a screen and reconstruct history, and "cartographic regression" overlays historical surveys, maps and aerial photographs onto modern satellite imagery to understand people and territory. "Photographic restitution" re-creates destroyed sites.

Identify, verify and amplify. Weizman's department hopes the work in Namibia leads to an investigative film, an interactive mapping platform, a contribution to legal case files and exhibitions in Germany, Namibia and

ABOVE: Forensic Architecture uses a 3D model to allow for the placement of soldiers and civilians based on activist footage to investigate an assault in Hebron, which was cross-referenced against the virtual testimonies of the witnesses

elsewhere. Weizman knows that films and exhibitions capture the attention of the wider public, who might not wade through lengthy reports.

Forensic Architecture and Bellingcat work with a patience that it is hard for most journalists, operating these days under a challenging economic model, to emulate. It will not replace the older ways, which have contemporaneous colour and protagonists offering their version of events. But they will tell you, after the dust settles, what actually happened. They set out not only to speak truth to power but also to produce irrefutable evidence. ✖

Sarah Sands is a trustee of Index and former editor of BBC Radio 4's Today

> As he put it at the time: The Press is dying, long live the news. Generations of journalists learned to ask: who, what, why, where and when? The Bellingcat motto is identify, verify, amplify

51(03):30/32 | DOI:10.1177/03064220221126397

Keeping the faith

Ahead of the release of his new book, the activist
BENEDICT ROGERS talks to **JEMIMAH STEINFELD**
about why being banned from China won't stop him

THE YEAR WAS 2012 and Benedict Rogers found himself in Liaoning Province, China, next to the North Korean border as part of ongoing work to help North Korean refugees. The trip had gone smoothly but that changed on the last night. Over dinner his friend - a missionary and aid worker - received a call to say the authorities were looking for them. Thus followed a mad dash, away from dinner, out of town and in the opposite direction of any checkpoints.

China has an awkward relationship with North Korea, treating it much like a little brother – sometimes annoying, ultimately family. This means that when

ABOVE: The activist Benedict Rogers

North Koreans escape to China (and many do, as the river separating the two countries is more porous than the heavily fortified crossing with South Korea), they're sent back immediately →

LEFT: Rogers (left) with Aung San Suu Kyi

→ if discovered. Helping escapees is an act of dissent.

And yet Rogers says that was not the reason the authorities were after them. Instead it was because of a visit they had made to one of the state-sanctioned churches in Liaoning, where he reckons the priest was suspicious that they were working with the illicit underground church.

This brush with the authorities remained just that. The following morning Rogers successfully boarded a flight.

Today he's speaking to me from the comfort of his London home. He tells me he's grateful that the assumption about the church was made. If the authorities had known about his helping refugees, things might have ended differently.

The anecdote is one of many in Roger's forthcoming book, The China Nexus: Thirty Years In and Around the Chinese Communist Party's Tyranny, which is published in October. In many ways the anecdote is emblematic of the book's theme – to chart the interrelationship of China and the Beijing-backed satellite dictatorships and to expose just how dire rights are within them, contrary to what their officials might claim.

Rogers' personal story, from his early time in China to his later high-profile work (he is CEO of Hong Kong Watch, to list just one of his many impressive hats), is like a mirror on the wider rights landscape. The book also features an introduction from Hong Kong activist Nathan Law and an interview with the Dalai Lama. The timing is

no coincidence: October 2022 should mark the end of China's President Xi Jinping's two terms in power. Only a constitutional change under his leadership means he won't be stepping down. He's effectively "emperor for life".

"It's timely in October because of the Party Congress. I think it's also timely because the western world – or the free world – is really starting to wake up to the challenges of the Chinese regime," said Rogers.

Rogers, who discovered Christianity at university and describes his faith as a factor motivating his human rights work, has been actively campaigning for three decades now. He believes the diplomatic dial has shifted, moved in part by the USA who are taking a more confrontational approach, as evidenced by their sanctions and the passage of the Uyghur Forced Labor Prevention Act. The UK is playing catch-up but at least they're finally playing. Rogers recounts an incident from 2016 to show just how much the mood has changed. It was the height of what was named the 'Golden Era' of UK-China relations, a label that says it all really, and Rogers was involved in producing a report for a UK parliamentary group on human rights in China.

"At the time the British government were furious at us because it was in their mind very unhelpful to the so-called Golden Era and there were very few MPs who were really willing to put their names out and put their heads above the parapet. That's changed dramatically now. There are lots of MPs on all sides who do speak out very strongly."

Rogers even cites the recent Conservative Party leadership race. China has come up as an issue for both candidates (Liz Truss just declared her intentions to designate China an "acute threat", for example).

Rogers' path into activism started in the early 90s when, aged 18, he headed

> ≡ At the time the British government were furious at us because it was in their mind very unhelpful to the so-called Golden Era

CREDIT: Benedict Rogers

off to Qingdao, a city in the north of China, to teach English as part of a year off before university.

He wanted to do something different, nay "meaningful". Once there, he soon became transfixed by the country. He reels off the clichés – the food, the history – as things he loved and then moves on to the people.

"I was made to feel very welcome. There was a real desire on the part of the people I got to know, a real eagerness, to engage with a foreigner. They were very keen to learn English, to have exchanges about our two cultures and countries."

He also talks about the acts of kindness he experienced, such as one time when he accidentally burnt his only pair of long johns in the middle of northern China's brutal winter. The mother of a friend sent him a new pair the next day.

"And there was this lovely note saying 'You've come from a long way away to teach us English and we should look after you and make sure you're not cold'," said Rogers.

From the moment Rogers arrived it became clear that human rights played a central role in China's political and social fabric. The massacre in Tiananmen Square had taken place a few years prior and people were talking about it.

"Despite being so soon after Tiananmen people were quite ready to talk about it politically, obviously only at home and in private conservations. I didn't go out there as an activist and nor to do what I do now but I was certainly aware and it did come into conversation quite often," he remarked.

It's strange to reflect on these conversations; today they probably wouldn't happen. China's grip on dissent has tightened under Xi. Combined with a new generation born after 1989, knowledge of the massacre is scant. Even if these conversations did take place, it might be a case of whether trees make sounds when they fall in the woods – they'd be hard to

On a national level, we need to unite – don't allow China to isolate countries

determine now for people working in the human rights field as many simply can't visit the country. Rogers is one of them. In addition to be denied entry to Hong Kong, something he discovered only once at the airport, he was charged earlier this year under Hong Kong's draconian national security law. If he was to return to China or its satellite states he'd likely end up in jail. Does this affect his advocacy?

"In the past I definitely worked with networks inside the country. In recent years it's much more the diaspora. And that's true of Myanmar, it's true of China itself and it's very much true of Hong Kong.

"It does mean that there can be a little bit of a time lag between something happening – not always, sometimes things happen and people can get information out quite quickly – and verifying what's happened or even learning about what's happened," he said, explaining that his advocacy before was based on what he called "the authenticity of first-hand experience and information", namely of being on the ground and able to discuss with media and parliament something he recently and directly experienced.

"Now I can't do that. It does present certain challenges and constraints," said Rogers, before adding, with conviction: "It doesn't mean one should stop."

Stop he won't. Despite the threats, sent to himself, his neighbours, even to his mother (who he assures me is very supportive and takes them in good humour) Rogers carries on with a steely determination.

We arrive at the future in our conversation and I'm keen to know what we, in the UK, can do. Rogers is clear. On a national level, we need to unite – don't allow China to isolate countries. On a more personal level, we have to

keep up the momentum. That means not letting the spotlight move on, which is something that has sadly happened with Tibet. Once a cause celebre, it's now (understandably but unhelpfully) dropped off the radar as attention has switched to the Uyghurs and Hong Kong. Then for the particularly pressing issues – Taiwan. We need to stand with them, albeit in an awkward balancing act whereby we do everything possible to prevent rather than provoke an invasion and a war. Finally, we should identify and team up with the diaspora living here.

It's a long list but if anyone models the power of advocacy it's Rogers. He's full of examples of his campaigning being successful, such as suggesting a visa scheme for Hong Kongers coming to the UK, something that the British government later adopted in 2020. That would not necessarily have been instituted when it was if "the ground hadn't been laid by our advocacy". It's these victories that keep him going, alongside the fortitude of others.

"I'm denied entry to Hong Kong, I can't go to China and Myanmar and I get a few threats but basically I'm safe, and free and comfortable," he told me and then contrasts this with those he campaigns for – people who live in daily fear, even outside China, and who often can't contact their families.

"They still keep going," said Rogers. "I'm left thinking 'I can't possibly give up if they haven't given up'." ✖

Benedict Rogers' new book The China Nexus: Thirty Years In and Around the Chinese Communist Party's Tyranny is published on 6 October 2022 by Optimum

Jemimah Steinfeld is editor-in-chief at Index

51(03):33/35|DOI:10.1177/03064220221126398

The double closet

ABOVE: A person holds a bisexual pride flag at a Pride march in London

Bi people are staying closeted in far higher proportions than other queer identities. **FLO MARKS** investigates why

IVING BEYOND TODAY'S largely accepted binaries of straight and gay, bisexual people can feel lonely and isolated. The label reminds them that others like them exist, but biphobia and erasure currently render their potential community largely invisible. As a bi woman myself, wanting to broaden understanding around the censored experience of bi people and highlight ways to embolden their freedom of expression, I asked other bi people to share their experiences in a psychologically safe space: 47 people from the UK provided detailed written responses. With many bi people's worst fear being publicly outed, respondents could remain anonymous, and all did.

Overall I found that bi people are self-censoring en masse, and staying closeted in far higher proportions than other queer (LGBTQ+) identities. This endorsed conclusions from the 2020 Stonewall Bi report, which stated that only one in five bi people were likely to be out to their families compared to three in five (63%) gay and lesbian people.

Some do not disclose their sexuality, feeling it is a private, need-to-know matter. As a South African 28-year-old bi woman, living in Hampshire, told Index, "I've never felt the need to come out as I don't feel straight should be the 'default' sexuality, but when it's relevant I do mention that I'm bisexual to people I am comfortable sharing this information with." Yet more concerning are those who mask and hide their identity from those they love, out of fear of potential consequences such as unsettling current relationships with family, friends, partners and colleagues. And, of equal worry is that bi people experience poor mental health, including, according to Stonewall, twice the amount of bi people self-harming compared to gay and lesbian people.

CREDIT: Ink Drop/Alamy

What are the reasons for this? An outdated UK educational system, exacerbated by unfavourable and unfair representation in the media, has led to ignorance of what it is to be bisexual and to nasty stereotypes being projected onto bi bodies; the latter translating into bi-phobic discrimination, bi-erasure and isolation of bi people from society[ies]. A 19-year-old bi woman from London told Index, "It can be frustrating and also damaging when people act like they know more about your sexuality than you do yourself."

Biphobia, hate and discrimination towards bi people because of their sexuality remains very real in the UK; and is amplified for those in the community who face intersectional discrimination due to other aspects of their identity such as being trans, disabled or from a minority ethnic group. This is particularly painful when it comes from loved ones. As a 19-year-old woman told Index, "an ex-partner of mine, in particular, was really harmful when he found out. He said 'You can't come out to people, because it would make them think I turned you.' That made me not want to share or be proud of who I am for a long time."

Widespread negative and gendered connotations of bi individuals being deviant, greedy or promiscuous enforce feelings that their sexuality is something to be ashamed of. They surface both in media representation and everyday language. This reinforces self-censorship. "The over-fetishisation of bisexuality [cited by many bi women respondents] has definitely made me question the romantic aspects of my sexuality and whether I feel romantically inclined as well as sexually," a 21-year-old woman told Index. And, she continued, "as an assumed straight person, I had to listen for years to the gay jokes and ridicules. If I had been out, I felt like they would have said this behind my back. It made me feel lonely and powerless."

Then there is bi-erasure. As a 22-year-old pansexual man (who is primarily attracted to personality, rather than gender) from Surrey told Index, "There are phrases that I have heard too many times to count - on the way to being gay, it's a phase, you're just experimenting, are you sure?, but you've never had sex with a guy?" Often unnoticed to a casual observer, or even the discriminator, phrases like these contribute to dismissing, devaluing and degrading bi experiences.

Accusations of bisexuality being a phase infers bi people are merely confused on their way to settling into a more permanent state of gay or straight. Depending on the gender you present, patriarchal norms determine which way you are assumed to go. Bi men are gay but are in hiding. Bi women are experimenting but are straight. A 20-year-old bi woman from Northern Ireland told Index, "I still don't feel validated. Often given the 'you aren't bi, you're straight and you just say you are bi for attention,' makes me hesitant to say anything at all."

A 21-year-old American bi woman told Index, "I started questioning at a young age, but I didn't know about bisexuality really (in the sense of being attracted to two or more genders) so I was super confused because I thought you had to be either straight or gay."

UK government research suggests biphobic bullying and erasure persists in schools, and that discussions of sexuality have been omitted; for the few who had received a formal education, only 9% said the content had prepared them for life as an LGBT person. When people invalidate bi-sexuality and contribute to an individual's self-censorship due to fears of being other and deviant, it can therefore sometimes be due to an awareness deficit rather than malice.

Unfortunately, biphobia and erasure can carry over into queer spaces, leading bi people to self-censor further. One 20-year-old Hong Kong-Chinese bi woman told Index, "If I am seen to be dating a male-presenting person I am straight and if I'm dating someone who is female-presenting then I'm gay, never just bisexual." And a 22-year-old pan man told Index, "I've had people look at me with suspicion when I've stated I'm pan, this has usually come from gay guys. Overall I've heard these comments and had these looks from queer, and heterosexual people so often that I barely notice them now."

This effectively creates a double closet where individuals feel their freedom of expression is compromised in both queer and straight settings, and they are reluctant to openly express their sexuality in either. Stonewall recently reported that 43% of their bi respondents had never attended an LGBTQ+ space. As one respondent told Index, "I feel like I don't always fit in. Because I'm too gay for heterosexual people and too straight for homosexual people."

Grappling with their identity, a prerequisite to bi people being more open, and feeling more valid in queer (and straight) spaces, is having had romantic and/or sexual experiences with multiple genders. "I don't feel 100% validated as I've never actually had experience with the same gender," a 20-year-old bi woman told Index. It becomes the ammunition to use against those who may dismiss them, or, even, helps them to overcome their own internalised bi-phobia. This is →

> Bi people experience poor mental health; over twice the amount of bi people self-harm compared to gay and lesbian people

"Sometimes gay women don't want to date bisexual women because they've been with a man, which hurts a lot," a 19-year-old woman told Index

→ regardless of the fact dating history and experiences are irrelevant to determining one's sexuality.

Pushing bi people away from LGBTQ+ spaces is due to a small minority who perpetuate toxic jokes and stereotypes that can further erode bi people's sense of belonging, legitimacy and ability to be open. One such is the "gold star" ideal where lesbian and gay men find pride or legitimacy in having never slept with the opposite gender; this isolates and rejects bi people who've had opposite-gender experiences. "Sometimes gay women don't want to date bisexual women because they've been with a man, which hurts a lot," a 19-year-old woman told Index. Another 21-year-old woman said she had overheard stories of "femme [feminine] presenting women being kicked out of gay clubs, even though they are attracted to women." And a 23-year-old bi woman told Index "I have lost some friends in the queer community who, although they say they are supportive, are not validating and don't perceive me as 'queer enough'." This does little to stem worries about being an imposter in queer circles.

Linked to the toxicity towards bi people in queer circles is the concept of them "not being gay enough". Distance is created between bi people and the LGBTQ+ community due to mainstream ideas about what constitutes the latter. As a 20-year-old bi woman told Index, "the LGBTQ+ community is a safe place for anyone and anything that exists outside of heteronormativity." However, with the majority of bi people being cis-gendered (same as birth) and in straight-presenting relationships, many bi people have been made to feel they conform a little too much to the heteronormativity. A 20-year-old Hong Kong-Chinese woman told Index that in the LGBTQ+ community some "people think your queer sexuality goes away if you're not with someone of the same gender."

Those in straight-presenting relationships have even been accused, on and offline, of having 'straight-passing privilege', the get-out-of-jail-free card to avoiding homophobia; a view dismissive of internal queer realities of bi people. Multiple respondents told Index they felt being in straight-presenting relationships, especially marriages, made them less likely to be welcomed in LGBTQ+ spaces, and therefore less likely to go. A 23-year-old bi woman, whose partner come out as trans part way through their relationship, told Index, "The fact it had to take what looked like a cishet [cis-gendered and hetereosexual/straight] relationship of people of differing genders (although both queer) to being an openly same sex queer couple for people to appreciate me being bisexual wasn't totally validating."

Sasha Misra, associate director of Communications and Campaigns at Stonewall, told Index: "Bi people are an important part of the LGBTQ+ acronym but their own experiences are often ignored, including within LGBTQ+ spaces. The erasure that bi people face often means that it's harder to be their full selves in daily life."

She continued: "Our community is stronger when we stand together against all the prejudices that affect lesbian, gay, bi, trans and queer people. We can't ignore the biphobia that is too prevalent in spaces that should be safe for bi people and must do more to challenge biphobia wherever we see it – even if that's within our own communities. There's still so much to do to ensure that all LGBTQ+ people are free to thrive as themselves, and bi equality is a vital part of that journey."

What is needed is a repositioning of and reframing of what constitutes the LGBTQ+ community where all identities can claim their space, inclusivity is paramount and freedom of expression emboldened. Pride, charities and formal social groups are vital, but the LGBTQ+ community must move away from being an exclusive club.

Finding comfort and empowerment in friends, and a more inclusive queer community also could help bi people lead more open lives. An American 20-year-old bi woman told Index, "I feel that being queer does make you closer to other queer people because we often have a common struggle we can relate to. I am happy that other closeted people have had the courage to talk to me about them questioning their sexuality because I am openly bi, and hopefully help them gain confidence in being who they are." It can be hugely validating and therapeutic to relate to similar experiences, as I did when reading the respondents' answers. That's not to say allies aren't also important. As a 21-year-old bi woman told Index, "I feel super lucky that I have such incredible straight friends who have been fundamental in me accepting who I am."

To achieve this, there must be far greater awareness of bi-identity[ies] and related issues in educational environments as well as in representation in the media.

With teaching LGBT curriculum now a legal obligation, the Department of Education (DoE) confirmed to Index that a school's provision of such is now part of Ofsted's school inspection handbook, and the DoE "has plans to monitor implementation of RSHE [Relationships, Sex and Health Education] over time." This qualitative research aims to test whether schools

Bi people shouldn't have to go down rabbit holes to find "their people"

are implementing RSHE sufficiently, whether it is improving outcomes for the children, and to understand the barriers and facilities to quality implementation.

"This wasn't a thing when I was at school and I think if it is taught, it will encourage people to be more accepting and understanding, and will stop children and teens searching up harmful things on the internet to try and figure out why they feel 'different'," said a 23-year-old from London.

Creating a more accurate and empowering representation of bi individuals on-screen and off-screen is also important. "The TikTok algorithm has worked out that I'm bi and non-binary, so my main connection to other LGBTQ+ people is via social media," a 20-year-old told Index. Although important, bi people shouldn't have to go down rabbit holes to find "their people". It must become more mainstream. Those in the media must not be erased, as the bisexuality of both Lady Gaga and David Bowie have been before (Gaga is often presented as an ally to the LGBTQ+ community, not a member, while Bowie's sexuality was the source of much controversy).

In film and TV, representation is important, especially when characters aren't just a token LGBTQ+ character but when they are an important storyline; this is needed for all genders,

ABOVE: Stephanie Beatriz (left) who is bisexual in real life and plays a bisexual character in the hit TV show Brooklyn Nine-Nine

but particularly for bi men and non-binary people. And, fundamentally, rather than characters being portrayed as sexy and free, having characters self-identify as bisexual, using that word, would be empowering. A powerful example of this was by the Brooklyn Nine-Nine star Rosa Diaz, portrayed by bisexual actor Stephanie Beatriz. She came out to her colleagues and friends saying, "There's something I'd like to say. I'm a pretty private person, so this is kind of hard for me but here we go. I'm bisexual." ✖

Flo Marks is a researcher at Index and a politics undergraduate

51(03):36/39|DOI:10.1177/03064220221126399

CREDIT: (Şercan) Press One/Article: Emilia Şercan: "State authorities have orchestrated a kompromat operation against me. Now they're trying to cover it up," published on Press One website on 04/04/2022; (Oprea) Wiktor Dabkows/Alamy

LEFT: Romanian reporter Emilia Şercan found out that powerful people in politics, the military and the secret services claimed to have doctorates in fields in which they had no knowledge

Is there a (real) doctor in the house?

Romanian politicians have been faking PhDs. **JOHN LLOYD** talks to the journalist who risked it all to expose them

ROMANIA, AMONG THE most totalitarian of the communist states in the post-war period under president Nicolae Ceauşescu, has – over the three decades since his death – developed a remarkable cadre of investigative journalists. That's true, to different degrees, in all post-communist societies – though in Russia and the Central Asian states they operate at their peril. In Romania, which can be described as "partially democratic", business moguls control most of the country's media and are tightly integrated with the political parties. Investigation is possible, but it quickly becomes a series of struggles to publish and to highlight abuse and corruption.

It has a champion in the Ratiu Family Charitable Foundation, named after Ion Ratiu, a liberal politician and presidential candidate, which annually presents awards for hard-driving, independent journalism – but cannot protect its awardees.

Ovidiu Vanghele, among the most audaciously probing of the investigators, calls the relationship with the state "tormented" and "crooked".

Along with Diana Ocioiu and Vlad Stoicescu, he unearthed widespread abuse of minors by a bishop of the Romanian Orthodox Church at a Christian high school – an investigation which continues and is being bitterly fought through the courts.

Among the most "tormented" of the investigations is that mounted – again, still with more to unearth – by Emilia

Şercan. Şercan, born in Vatra Dornei, in the north-eastern corner of Romania, has in a 25-year career reported, or led investigative teams to report, on the many darker corners of Romanian politics and business. In the course of that career, she frequently found her weeks or months of work discarded for being too uncomfortable to business or political interests, or published in small circulation media with the larger media refusing to pick up the story.

Slight and courteous, she has, in pursuit of a story which reached into the very top of her country's politics, shown a stubborn and bold spirit which shames the subjects of her story and a swathe of the Romanian establishment. A part-time academic – she teaches journalism technique at the University of Bucharest – she became aware that senior figures in politics, the military and the secret services were acquiring doctorates (PhDs) in areas of study where they had no expertise or history.

She began digging and learned that universities affiliated to the Ministry of Defence, the Interior Ministry and the Romanian Intelligence Service all had doctoral programmes and were awarding doctorates to politicians, judges, police officers and high-ranking civil servants. Why, she asked, go there when they could go to civil universities with a larger choice of disciplines and more highly qualified scholars?

When, with difficulty, she found content in many of the theses had been plagiarised it became clear what was happening.

She said: "These military universities were, practically speaking, a production line for the development of the

A doctorate isn't required to get to the top, but it attracts a higher salary

plagiarism phenomenon in Romania. They always operated in a hermetic system, there was never any real civilian control over these universities, as there is, in fact, none over the Romanian Intelligence Service or even over the entire intelligence system in Romania."

Her investigations reached the top of politics. In 2015, she published evidence that Gabriel Oprea, the interior minister and a former army general – and, briefly, prime minister in that year – had, when a university professor and doctoral supervisor, plagiarised wildly for his own doctoral thesis.

She also uncovered a network of politicians, magistrates and senior state officials, all supervised by Oprea, who had plagiarised the content of their doctoral theses. Oprea protested that the allegation was false and that he was the victim of a political vendetta. An inquiry found this to be false, further scandals relating to decisions he had made erupted and, bit by bit, he was forced out.

A doctorate isn't required to get to the top, but it attracts a higher salary and it confers status. There's even a malign example from the past: Elena Ceaușescu, the dictator's wife and a power in her own right, had a PhD in chemistry faked for her, and was lauded for it in the communist-era media. Universities and institutes abroad were pressed to entertain her as a distinguished scholar.

Drawn into a world of deception which has proven hydra-headed, Șercan reported on the fake PhD theses of several high-ranking police officers – and was rewarded by death threats from a police academy official named Adrian Barbulescu. As the prosecutors discovered, Barbulescu had been directed to issue the threats by Adrian Iacob, rector of the Police Academy,

Șercan reported on the fake PhD theses of several high-ranking police officers – and was rewarded by death threats

and his pro-rector Petrica Mihail Marcoci. Iacob and Marcoci were found guilty of blackmailing Șercan and were sentenced by the Supreme Court to three-year suspended sentences, losing the right to be police officers and university professors.

Her latest, and highest, quarry is the present prime minister, Nicolae Ciucă – also a former army general – who took office in November last year. Șercan discovered that almost one-third of his thesis had been plagiarised. Ciucă excused himself by saying that the doctorate was "drawn up in accordance with the legal requirements of the time".

Ciucă remains in post, and Șercan continues to probe – but at a cost. Accustomed to working quietly and without fanfare, earlier this year she decided to speak out about the campaigns of defamation and intimidation that she faced – which became more severe after she revealed Ciucă's PhD plagiarism.

More serious, and seriously intimidating, is that her complaints appear to have been followed by leaks from the police themselves, including photographs taken by her then-fiancé of her emerging from a shower.

In a detailed document, she wrote: "The key player is the Romanian state itself. A piece of evidence I provided to the Romanian police, with the end goal of identifying someone who had perpetrated a violation of privacy, was leaked from the criminal file that very same day and became the basis of an extensive kompromat operation."

Investigative reporters work under periodically intense pressure. They cannot continue to work, however, if the forces of law take the sides of those who wish to shut them down, or wish themselves to do so. Șercan's stubborn courage has done much to illuminate dark spaces, but she will need support from within Romania and outside to continue. ✖

John Lloyd is a contributing editor of the Financial Times

51(03):40/41|DOI:10.1177/03064220221126400

RIGHT: Gabriel Oprea, the Interior Minister of Romania and a former army general, plagiarised his own doctoral thesis in university, according to journalist Emilia Șercan

CREDIT: Robert Harding/Alamy

The mice hear the words of the night

JIHYUN PARK escaped from North Korea – twice. Now living in the UK, she reflects on the dangers of silence

WHEN I WAS a child in North Korea, I was brainwashed. Not only by my parents but also at school. (Later, as a schoolteacher, I trampled on freedom of speech and expression by brainwashing the next generation.)

One day, our teacher lined us up class by class and led us to a river. The bridge was the best place for the execution of a traitor as a huge crowd could gather below.

Once the hooded man, who could barely walk, was brought out of a car and tied to a post, the crowd shouted excitedly.

I couldn't hear what the soldiers

said, and after their shots rang out and the man's blood spilled I didn't feel sad. But as the car containing his body disappeared into the distance, it dawned on me that anyone could be executed.

Everyone stayed in place until we were granted permission to leave. I desperately wanted to speak, as did everyone around me, but silence was the only option. We went home, ate dinner as usual, and went to bed.

Living in North Korea, I remember being taught propaganda and incitement phrases such as "Let's beat the US imperialist wolf", "One-hearted unity" and "Self-reliance". Even if I'd understood what was wrong or right

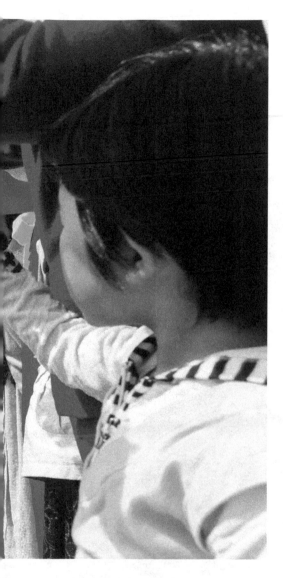

ABOVE: A military parade takes place in 2012 during celebrations on the 100th anniversary of the birth of President Kim Il Sung, in Pyongyang, North Korea

about it, I still couldn't say a word.

Our parents always told us: "A bird hears the words of the day, and the mice hear the words of the night." Words could be unforgiveable so, instead, we were taught to say nothing.

The people of North Korea, which has a secularist ideology, cannot say a bad word about the ruling Kim family. When Kim Jong-un first took power in 2011, after his father Kim Jong-il died, North Koreans were not allowed to ask

questions about him. Instead, they had to believe the official press releases. If they did ask questions, they would likely be sent to concentration camps – or simply disappear.

We never knew the words "dictator", "murderer" or "attacker". We didn't have language for human rights violations, freedom, women's rights or homosexuality. This might seem like basic vocabulary that can be used anywhere in the world, but foreign languages were never allowed in our mouths. We could use only words approved by the Kim dynasty.

North Koreans are nothing short of modern-day slaves who have been deprived of freedom of expression and movement, as well as all the universal rights that humans deserve.

Even when you name new-born babies you must name them in the North Korean way. If you use the names of famous South Korean actors, you will be subject to punishment in labour camps.

North Koreans should sing only North Korean songs. Not even songs from the South Korean band BTS, loved the world over, are allowed. Now, I listen to whatever music I wish to and my children sing freely.

Living in the UK, I am able to express "yes" or "no" clearly and I have the right to criticise the government for doing things wrong. But does living in a free democracy mean everyone can speak freely?

Article 19 of the Universal Declaration of Human Rights declares that freedom of expression is a common human right irrespective of borders. Although freedom of expression is a fundamental right, unlimited freedom is not guaranteed.

Like myself, there are many immigrants and refugees living in the UK, and the languages they speak are diverse. People who have settled in the UK work hard to learn English but grasping the language can be difficult. For those without good English language skills, their lives are getting worse. It's

We didn't have language for human rights violations, freedom, women's rights or homosexuality

as if they are standing at the foot of a steep hill. They're struggling to learn English and without it they are losing the opportunity to speak out against persecution and discrimination. They are losing their courage and confidence and so they are being punished further.

North Korea is a place where I lived like a machine and remained silent, even though I now know that silence causes persecution. North Korea is the real 1984. And silence is one of the most feared weapons, anywhere in the world.

Women who are violated and sexually assaulted online, or within the family, cannot defend themselves legitimately. They lose their freedom of expression because they remain silent.

But, for those without power, speech is one of the few weapons available. No matter how many rights are given, if you don't use them, they rust. Freedom of expression needs to be practised consistently and people should get used to it. The controversial few will have to face the furnace of public opinion and debate. The higher the level of this debate, the more nourishment for democracy.

All beliefs are universal human rights, and human dignity is paramount. ✖

Jihyun Park is a UK-based activist who defected from North Korea. She recently co-authored her memoir, The Hard Road Out

51(03):42/43|DOI:10.1177/03064220221126401

The most dangerous man in Guantanamo

The only journalist detained in Guantanamo, **SAMI ALHAJ**, tells **KATIE DANCEY-DOWNS** about his time there and how he's now fighting for a fallen friend

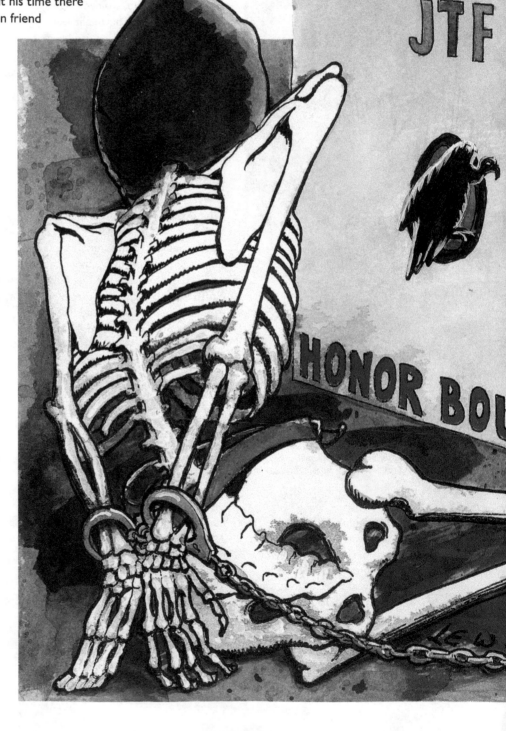

S AMI ALHAJ IS the only journalist who has reported from inside a Guantanamo Bay cell.

In this notorious US prison, the media is not welcome. Except, that is, for the Al Jazeera cameraman who was locked in a cell for six years and labelled as Prisoner 345. Now, he is turning his attention to other silenced journalists.

Guantanamo Bay, an area in Cuba which is home to a US-controlled naval base and detention camp, was set up in the wake of the 9/11 terror attacks to play grim host to suspected al-Qaeda members.

Alhaj claims the interrogators who picked him up in Pakistan admitted to having the wrong man before he was sent there. Another man went by the same name, and he believes that right from the get-go they made a mistake.

This mistake changed the course of his life. Torture and racist taunts were a staple of Guantanamo, all of which Alhaj was subjected to. Letters in and →

> Al Jazeera people face problems everywhere, especially in the Middle East, because they tell the truth

PICTURED: A recreation of a drawing by Sami Alhaj, which he created inside Guantanamo but which was barred from leaving the prison

→ out of Guantanamo were defaced by the censor's pen.

When Alhaj's son received a grade at school, the result was blanked out. Every number was erased. His lawyers got hold of the two versions, shaking their heads as they compared original correspondences with over-zealous redactions. Trying to find some humour in it all, they tested the boundaries on what would get past the prison gate – Jack and the Beanstalk was firmly rejected, lest Alhaj get the idea of planting a magic legume as a means of escape.

At some stage he claims he was asked to be a spy. "When they sent me to Guantanamo, some lady came and told me, 'Sami, we want to start the training with you'," Alhaj told Index. Over several meetings, Alhaj said he was asked to work with intelligence services. They wanted him to be an inside man in Al Jazeera, reporting back to US authorities in exchange for his freedom.

Alhaj is not the only person to make claims of this nature. Anonymous US officials have previously described a secret programme by the CIA to turn prisoners into double agents – a claim on which the CIA has not commented.

Alhaj rejected the offer and continued to do so every time he was asked.

Al Jazeera supported Alhaj throughout, publishing regular stories on his case, and he fed out stories about his fellow prisoners through his lawyer.

"He [his lawyer] told me, 'You are lucky to be in Guantanamo'," Alhaj said.

Not only were journalists not usually allowed in but Alhaj's disobedience would surely make them rethink locking up reporters in the future.

"He was the single most dangerous person in Guantanamo, because of everything we were accomplishing every day," Clive Stafford Smith, Alhaj's lawyer and the founder of human rights organisation Reprieve, told Index. "And that was the point. That's why he was released."

Alhaj spent 2,330 days in Guantanamo. Being targeted fuelled a

Abu Akleh wasn't scheduled to work on the day of her death. In a cruel act of fate, she switched to the very day she was killed

fire within him to fight for the protection of other journalists. Alhaj is now the director of the Al Jazeera Public Liberties and Human Rights Centre. Originally set up in 2008, its mission is threefold: human rights-focused editorials, partnerships with other organisations, and press freedom. All three sections work to protect journalists – specifically in the Middle East.

Alhaj helps create partnerships with NGOs to protect journalists and offers training and memberships to organisations. When journalists are under threat, it is documented.

"Al Jazeera people face problems everywhere, especially in the Middle East, because they tell the truth," Alhaj said. Those people include Atwar Bahjat and Yasser Bahjat, who were arrested by US troops in Baghdad in 2003. In 2016, Al Jazeera news producer Mahmoud Hussein was arrested while on holiday in Cairo, then held for four years without trial. Many more have been arrested, injured or killed.

"In the Middle East, there is no freedom of speech," Alhaj said. "The systems there are dictatorships. So, whoever writes or makes any reports against the government, they put him in jail."

Twelve Al Jazeera journalists have been killed while reporting. The latest of these is Shireen Abu Akleh, a Palestinian-American journalist killed while covering an Israeli security operation at the Jenin refugee camp in May. A UN Human Rights Office report concluded that "the shots that killed Abu Akleh and injured her colleague Ali Sammoudi came from Israeli Security Forces and not from indiscriminate firing by armed Palestinians". The UN

high commissioner is now urging Israeli authorities to open a criminal investigation.

Alhaj is working behind the scenes, fighting for justice for Abu Akleh. Given that she was a US national, Alhaj wants US authorities to investigate the death of his friend and colleague fully.

At the end of May, Al Jazeera's legal team referred Abu Akleh's case to the prosecutor of the International Criminal Court. Around 50 days after her death, the centre ran a symposium in Geneva to launch a campaign seeking justice for her, where Alhaj announced that Al Jazeera had formed a global legal alliance. A month later, the slain journalist's brother, Anton, and his daughter Lina met US secretary of state Antony Blinken. They renewed their demand for a thorough investigation and rejected attempts to close the file.

"We're looking for pressure from authorities," Alhaj said. "Nobody knows who killed her."

As he talks about the tragic loss, Alhaj explains how Abu Akleh wasn't scheduled to work on the day of her death but needed to clear another day for an upcoming visit from her brother. In a cruel act of fate, she switched to the very day she was killed.

Alhaj wants answers and justice for his friend, but he also wants protection for other journalists at risk. Journalists who are using their voices to tell the world important truths, and who risk their lives with every report. He knows the threat of silencing all too well. ✖

Katie Dancey-Downs is assistant editor at Index

51(03):44/46|DOI:10.1177/03064220221126402

America's coolest members club

As book banning surges in the USA, people are finding ways to read illicit literature, reports **OLIVIA SKLENKA**

KING'S BOOKS, LOCATED in Tacoma, Washington state, holds a virtual monthly book club with a twist. Known as the Banned Book Club, the members read books that have been banned or challenged – typically at schools or in school libraries.

And to further combat the stigma against the titles, the one selected is then made available to buy in the shop.

"You're able to learn about other people and their opinions through the books," club co-ordinator David Raff told Index.

Raff, who said the club was attended by people of all ages, added that the topics varied month-to-month.

ABOVE: A protest against book censorship in classrooms and libraries in Texas. Protesters sit in the Capitol rotunda and read some of the 850 books on a Republican lawmaker's list of "uncomfortable" titles

"You end up talking about topics that don't normally come up in conversation because banned books cover those controversial topics [including] the clichéd things you don't talk about in public."

This is just one of many initiatives around the USA to fight the rise in book banning. According to PEN's Banned in the USA report, 1,586 books were banned between 1 July 2021 and →

Just because a book is objectionable to a person doesn't mean that it should be banned to all

→ 31 March 2022. The report further states that book bans have occurred in 86 school districts in 26 states during this time. Those districts represent a "combined enrolment of more than two million students".

Other grassroots efforts include #FReadom, a campaign which started in Texas in which librarians tweet about books that are being targeted and describe their positive impact on students.

Carlyn Foote, one of the founders, is a retired librarian who lives in the state and is fighting back against attempted censorship.

"[The censorship effort] was so clearly targeting LGBTQ students," Foote told CNN. "It was so clearly targeting race. I just don't want students to feel like they are less than. That's what brought me to this."

Parents and students have also taken a stand against the regulations. According to the State of America's Libraries Special Report, "students at the Central York High School in southern Pennsylvania protested to reinstate materials that had been removed from their library's collection, including a children's book about Rosa Parks, Malala Yousafzai's autobiography and CNN's Sesame Street town hall on racism". Organisations have donated banned books to a plethora of establishments to ensure accessibility, and many parents have hosted protests in states

including Texas and Florida. Efforts to ban books might be growing, but so too is the pushback.

It goes without saying that book banning is problematic, and that reading, particularly about subjects outside of our own experiences, fosters understanding knowledge. But in the USA it's particularly targeted.

As wars over culture and ideology rage, many authors have found themselves, or rather their titles, in the crossfire. Topics about the LGBTQ community or from minority writers are frequently on the lists. Common titles include Racial Justice in America: Topics for Change by Hedreich Nichols, The Girls I've Been by Tess Sharpe, Cinderella is Dead by Kalynn Bayron, Understanding Gender by Juno Dawson, and Gender Equality by Marie Léonard.

Conservative politicians, public figures and groups have sought to eradicate any knowledge of those with diverse intersectional backgrounds and identities. Outspoken conservative groups believe that schools are forcing topics such as race theory and gender on children.

But, as many will highlight, these efforts are in conflict with the First Amendment of the US constitution, which guarantees the right to freedom of expression and includes the rights to read and learn.

Vera Eidelman, a lawyer with the American Civil Liberties Union, told the American Library Association: "Book bans in school and public libraries – places that are central to our abilities to explore ideas, encounter new perspectives and learn to think for ourselves – are misguided attempts to try to suppress that right."

Stephanie Hlywak, director of the American Library Association, wrote in its latest report: "Banning books won't make these realities and lived experiences disappear, nor will it erase our nation's struggles to realise true equity, diversity and inclusion. That's why the work of libraries is more

From public school libraries to commercial shelves

Libraries are not the only shelves that have come under attack in recent months

Bookshop chain Barnes & Noble made headlines when Tim Anderson, Republican state delegate in Virginia, brought fantasy novel A Court of Mist and Fury by Sarah J Maas and the memoir Gender Queer by non-binary cartoonist Maia Kobabe to court. Anderson claimed the books showcased material that was obscene and inappropriate for minors and wanted them to be sold only with parental permission.

Judge Pamela Baskervill ruled that "there is probable cause to believe" both books were "obscene for unrestricted viewing by minors".

According to Virginia state law, a judge can issue a temporary restraining order that prevents "the sale or distribution of the book alleged to be obscene".

With Anderson actively advocating for those two novels to be removed from shelves, only time will tell if the temporary restraining order will make it illegal to produce the books or to sell them to minors without their parental consent.

As it stands, allowing access to these books for teenagers without parental consent would implicate a variety of individuals, including any Barnes & Noble staff members.

essential than ever. Books reach across boundaries and build connections between readers."

Likewise, Raff believes that "just because a book is objectionable to a person doesn't mean that it should be banned to all". ✖

Olivia Sklenka is an intern at Index

51(03):47/48|DOI:10.1177/03064220221126403

SPECIAL REPORT

"We would like to tell the world that the dictator's hosting of the World Cup 2022 in our country is solely for the purpose of polishing and boosting the image of his precarious, corrupt, terrorist regime"

ABDULLAH AL-MALIKI | STADIUMS BUILT ON SUFFERING, P.53

Victim of its own success?

Football's popularity makes it appealing to populists. We shouldn't overlook how it unites and gives a voice to many, writes **SIMON BARNES**

FOOTBALL IS A bit like post-impressionist painting: both are thrilling, beautiful and packed with meaning, and both have been bought up by the state of Qatar. Among the top five most expensive paintings ever bought are Cezanne's The Card Players and Gauguin's When Will You Marry? Qatar paid US$550 million for them.

The men's football World Cup will be held in Qatar at the end of the year and will cost the state rather more: an estimated US$220 billion. It's been reported that more than 6,500 migrant workers have died since construction of the eight stadiums began. Qatar has an infamous human rights record; homosexuality is illegal and the oppression of women is a matter of routine.

It's called sportswashing. The word revels in glorious sport, associates the thrill, beauty and meaning with the host nation and forgets all about the nation's darker side. It's not a new idea. Russia held the previous World Cup in 2018; Abu Dhabi took over Manchester City in 2008 and created a team of fascinatingly brittle beauty; Qatar bought Paris St Germain in 2011 and filled it with glamour signings; the Saudi sovereign wealth fund acquired Newcastle United last year.

Football has long been used to make unlikely people look good. English football clubs were traditionally owned

PICTURED: Russian President Vladimir Putin and Fifa president Gianni Infantino present the trophy to France after the final of the 2018 World Cup, which was held in Russia

by the local dodgy builder or the town's brewer; now they're more often owned by gambling interests. It's about both vanity and profit. Classic example: Roman Abramovich owned Chelsea from 2003 to this year, when he was forced to sell up because of Russia's invasion of Ukraine; it made him a global figure.

It's an ugly tradition. But Qatar's involvements in football doesn't make football ugly any more than Qatar's investment in post-impressionism makes the work of Cezanne and Gaugin ugly.

Football is much loved across the world – and also much despised. There are two usual reasons for the despising: social snobbery and intellectual snobbery. Football is traditionally the game of the poor: I have often watched barefoot games in Africa with a ball made from a million plastic bags. You need rather more for the sports of the elite.

The intellectual's aversion to football is based on the principle that stupid people like football, so if you hate football you must be clever. (Point of information: stupid people also like

sex.) Intellectual disdain for football as a form of philistinism: the fact that you can appreciate the Dutch Total Football team of 1974 doesn't disqualify you from enjoying Ulysses.

The practice of sportswashing is another reason to despise the game. But football is capable of doing good things. Sporting ability is obvious and unmistakable, which makes sport pretty egalitarian. Throughout the 1960s no one doubted that Pelé of Brazil was the best footballer in the world. His speed of thought and body, his skill and his

intelligence were blindingly obvious: a black man admired across the world to the point of veneration.

The process continues: football constantly throws up heroes from all races and backgrounds. France won the World Cup in 1998 thanks to the brilliance of Zinedine Zidane of North African extraction; they won again in

2018 and their top players were Kylian Mbappe and N'Golo Kante.

Football is the world's Esperanto, the one global passport. I have discussed football with strangers on six continents. I used to play regularly against Chinese teams when I lived in Hong Kong: a better bond than my Cantonese or their English.

This summer the England women's ➔

Football has long been used to make unlikely people look good

→ football team won the European Championship, and the final was watched by 17 million people, not a bad result for feminism. Oscar Wilde said: "Football is all very well as a game for rough girls, but it is hardly suitable for delicate boys." The whole tournament was a glorious celebration of rough girls.

Sport depends for its existence on a paradox: it is trivial in itself, but played and watched as if it actually mattered. From this come vivid revelations of

Sport is something people want, and so people want to control it

human beings in conflict. It was once believed that sport was good because it built character; these days we believe sport is good because it reveals character.

As novels, plays and films bring us significant incidents that reveal great truths, so does sport. Example: in 1986 when Argentina played England, Diego

Maradona scored a goal with his hands, unabashed urchin cheating. He followed this with a run through England's entire defence, still remembered by some as the greatest goal of all time: a classic demonstration of flawed greatness.

Football takes hold of people's imagination. It's been called the working man's ballet. Speed, skill, cheating, triumph, disaster, despair, redemption: all these things can be found in a single football match. That's why people follow the game. That's why the floating voters watch half a match in the World Cup and get sucked in, watching to the bitter end. It often starts with partisanship, but sport can take you to lofty levels of excellence: and the pursuit of excellence can never be entirely trivial.

Sport is something people want, and so people want to control it. That's why Hitler staged the Olympic Games in Berlin in 1936. Football, the most popular of all games, runs deep in human nature, and those who take control of football believe they control much of humanity. Football is no more a good thing than a bad thing, but like everything else – including great art – it is frequently put to bad use.

In the end, football is a sunflower. Sunflowers are beautiful. Van Gogh painted them and by doing so he taught us about the marvellous nature of the ordinary. BP uses a sunflower emblem for greenwashing: to convince us that the more we use petroleum the faster we will move into a green and pleasant future.

We don't blame the sunflower for this. We shouldn't blame football for the ways it is exploited. But if we are not aware of them we allow the exploiters to take us for fools. ✖

Simon Barnes is former chief sports writer of The Times

51(03):50/52|DOI:10.1177/03064220221126404

Political football

Controversy has always surrounded World Cups, writes GUILHERME OSINSKI

1934 Italy
In the second World Cup in history, Italian dictator Benito Mussolini did everything he could to guarantee the trophy would stay in Italy. First, he used the event to showcase the Italian fascist regime, and then invited South American players, such as Argentinians Luís Monti, Raimundo Orsi and Brazilian Filó, to play for the Italian side. They won.

1938 France
The last World Cup before World War II took place in France. Nazi Germany recruited five Austrian players to join their side, who each wore a swastika on their kits. But Matthias Sindelar, arguably the most important Austrian player at the time, declined to play. When Germany faced Switzerland, they initially took an early 2-0 lead, which vanished in the second half when Switzerland scored four goals to win the match. Many believe the Austrian players lost it on purpose. One year later, Sindelar was found dead in his home.

1978 Argentina
Argentina hosted the World Cup when it was under a bloody military dictatorship which persecuted trade unionists, students, journalists and anyone suspected of being socialist or against the regime. All of this sparked protests. In Paris, for example, French and Argentine activists created the COBA (Committee to Boycott the Cup in Argentina).

1998 France
The most talked about match of the 1998 World Cup was Iran versus United States. Tensions had been high between both country since the American hostage crisis in Tehran in 1979, and the USA's support of Iraq in the war against Iran. Ali Khamenei, Iran's supreme leader, wanted his team to take to the field with a spirit of war. Instead Iranian players came with flowers and offered them to the Americans, in a symbolic gesture for peace and human rights.

2014 Brazil
Many Brazilians were not happy about hosting the World Cup, leading to major popular protests. Known as "Fifa go Home", the cities that hosted the matches were filled with protesters indignant that public money was being allocated to the construction of stadiums, instead of essential public services such as hospitals and schools.

2019 Women's World Cup, France
In 2017, women's football legend Ada Hegerberg informed the Norwegian Federation that she would no longer participate in the sport until women were treated fairly and on a par with men's football in the country. Then in 2019 she refused to participate in the World Cup in France. In an interview with ESPN in 2019, Hegerberg said: "I feel like I was placed in a system where I didn't have a voice. I felt this weight on my shoulders more and more: This isn't working."

Stadiums built on suffering

Qatari activist **ABDULLAH AL-MALIKI** makes an emotional plea to not watch the World Cup

T IS UNFORTUNATE, to say the least, that the 2022 Football World Cup is hosted by the oppressive dictatorial regime of my country, the State of Qatar.

The regime – led by the dictator Tamim bin Hamad Khalifa al-Thani, his terrorist gang and his immediate family – controls the judiciary, the legislative and the executive authorities as well as all print and audio-visual media, including the state-owned Al Jazeera satellite channel. It also controls the gas and oil resources of the Qatari people, prohibits peaceful freedom of expression and imposes harsh life sentences on those who criticise or oppose it.

This dictatorial regime has even gone so far as to demand the execution of peaceful Qatari activists because they exposed its human rights violations and spoke out against its corruption.

It is a disgrace to humanity that this dictatorial regime should be hosting the 2022 World Cup. Is it reasonable for the event to be hosted by those who violate the human rights of Qataris inside and outside of Qatar, as well as the rights of migrant workers in Qatar? Is it reasonable for the World Cup to be organised on the back of the regime's support for terrorism and extremism, particularly in Libya and Syria?

The regime is deliberately keeping the Qatari people ignorant on the political, security and economic matters of the state and prevents them from monitoring its actions. In 2021, the regime tried to deceive the world with a parliament whose members were, they said, two-thirds elected by the people, and one-third appointed by Tamim. This is nothing but deception. The elected two-thirds are all civil servants, and the appointed one-third is equally made up of civil servants. The regime also

prevented more than half the population from voting and from running for office on the pretext that they were second, third and fourth class citizens. This is the height of the farce.

Moreover, this parliament (the Shura Council) has no oversight on political, security and economic matters, according to the law decreed by Tamim in 2021.

All those who have criticised its backward, racist laws have been incarcerated, as have all those who assembled peacefully to protest against them.

This regime is trying to convince the world that it is civilised and that it respects human rights and spreads peace in the world. The truth is that it is deceitful, with no credibility. Any time it has intervened in another country it has brought about destruction and given rise to terrorism. The clearest evidence for this is the its interventions in Libya, Syria, Egypt, Lebanon, Sudan and Yemen, where it has caused humanitarian disasters and displacement.

It is a regime without the slightest sense of responsibility; a regime that thinks it can buy people and everything else with money. In 2011, for example, Qatar sent forces to Libya without the consent of the Qatari people, and those forces committed murder, terrorism and other crimes against men, women and children.

And it has turned against its own people, too. Qatar has been revoking

ABOVE: Tamim bin Hamad Khalifa al-Thani pictured in Doha in February 2020

citizenship of thousands of citizens from the al-Murrah tribe and others since 1996. This is a policy based on the practice of exclusion, marginalisation and punishment of the Qatari people. It went so far as to revoke citizenship of more than 6,000 Qatari citizens from the tribe between 2004 and 2005, expelling them from their homes and depriving them of electricity, water, healthcare and education.

Some were thrown over the Saudi border and those living abroad were denied entry to Qatar.

In 2003 the State Security Agency was established, which was granted extensive powers to do whatever it wanted inside and outside Qatar, thus becoming above the country's law. It files lawsuits against Qatari activists and calls for their →

> ## It is a disgrace to humanity that this dictatorial regime should be hosting the 2022 World Cup

PICTURED: Workers walk past building work on the Khalifa International Stadium in Doha, Qatar. Migrant workers have faced awful conditions in the country

→ execution because they criticise the regime and demand respect for human rights and democracy in their country.

The regime categorically rejects all calls for democracy or the peaceful transfer of power. Anyone who makes such demands is considered its enemy – someone who deserves the death penalty or life imprisonment.

They work in tandem with Qatari embassies abroad, who refuse to renew the passports of liberal-minded Qatari citizens and human rights activists.

We are dealing with a regime that does not believe in peaceful coexistence with those of different opinions, as evidenced by the presence of Qatari citizens abroad who cannot return home out of fear for their safety because of their peaceful expression of opinions. Their inevitable fate would be life imprisonment or execution.

These sentences prove to the world the extent to which the politicised

judiciary in Qatar is rotten and corrupt.

The ruling regime has imprisoned and banned from travel all Qatari human rights defenders who come under suspicion for their peaceful human rights activities, including, for example, leading Qatari human rights activist Muhammad bin Yousef al-Sulaiti,

human rights activist and international coordinator Abdullah bin Ahmed Bumatar al-Muhannadi, international human rights lawyer Najib bin Muhammad al-Nuaimi, lawyers Hazza al-Marri and Rashed al-Marri, writer Abdullah al-Salem al-Marri, activists Muhammad bin Mahras al-Marri, Latifa Al-Mosefri and Nouf Al-Maadid, writer Mohammed bin Abdulrahman al-Thani, and citizens Turki bin Ali al-Arabid al-Shahwani, Saud bin Khalifa al-Thani and Issa bin Mardi al-Shammari.

On 21 July, Qatari State Security carried out a large-scale operation where they kidnapped Abdullah bin Ahmed Bumatar al-Muhannadi, as well as Issa bin Mardi al-Shammari and Saud bin Khalifa al-Thani.

Innocent people are murdered by the regime, including Fahd bin Ahmed al-Bohendi, killed in prison in 2020. An international investigation committee should be set up to look into this murder, because the investigations held here cannot be trusted.

In view of this, how can you not boycott the 2022 World Cup in Qatar? Tamim bin Hamad al-Thani and his father, Hamad bin Khalifa al-Thani, before him enacted laws that served their interests and allowed them to stay in power for life. Laws that give them powers to do what they want with the Qatari people and the expatriates, to seize the wealth of the Qatari people, and to practise, support and fund terrorism.

Tamim has planted fear and terror in the hearts and minds of the Qatari people. No one in our country can criticise the actions and words of the corrupt dictator, or those of his terrorist gang.

We would like to tell the world that the dictator's hosting of the World Cup 2022 in our country is solely for the purpose of polishing and boosting the image of his precarious, corrupt, terrorist regime, and not for the sake of human civilisation or the development of football in our region and indeed in the world.

> The football stadiums that were built in our country were built on the corpses of migrant workers and the stolen wealth of the Qatari people

The football stadiums that were built in our country, the State of Qatar, were built on the corpses of migrant workers and the stolen wealth of the Qatari people, and on the suffering from human rights violations.

How can a decent, liberal person agree to attend the World Cup and accept that it is hosted by the State of Qatar, in the shadow of the crimes, terrorism, corruption and violations committed by the current dictatorial regime? A rejection of Qatar's hosting of the 2022 World Cup would be an explicit rejection of these violations.

The state of Qatar cannot continue to deceive the people, or the countries of the world, with its fake and flashy slogans. The decent and free people of Qatar are determined to establish a pluralistic democratic system which is based on the protection, respect and defence of human rights. This noble goal will only be achieved when the regime is peacefully overthrown. This is a matter of time. We will never give up on our noble goal or take a single step back: in fact, we become more determined to achieve this goal every day. ✖

Abdullah al-Maliki is a Qatari human rights activist. He currently lives outside the country

51(03):53/55|DOI:10.1177/03064220221126405

Football's leaving home

When the Taliban took over in 2021, **KHALIDA POPAL** was instrumental in getting footballers out of Afghanistan. She tells **KATIE DANCEY-DOWNS** about the beginning and end of women's football in the country

KHALIDA POPAL TAKES the trophies for both bringing women's football to Afghanistan and for evacuating the beating heart of the game in the face of the Taliban takeover. Popal, the first captain of the Afghan women's football team, was also one of the founding members of the league at a time when women simply did not play the game in the country. Having such a prominent image, however, comes with risks.

Popal remembers organising a friendly game between Afghan women footballers and female Nato soldiers, and how death threats became a fixture in her life soon after. She feared attacks not only from the Taliban but from anyone who supported their ideology.

"Many times I was attacked. Physically, I was harassed. And it was so dangerous for me to continue living in that country," she told Index over the phone from Copenhagen, where she now lives. (She left Afghanistan in 2011, finding safety in Denmark via refugee centres.)

Her stand against Taliban ideology meant she was branded as being brainwashed by the West, which put her in real danger. Popal left not just for her physical safety but so that she could continue speaking her mind.

"Football for me was a source of activism," she said, explaining how it was much the same for other female players in the country. "My purpose was to take action for inclusion of women in society."

Football was the activists' tool for standing together, and developing skills on the pitch often took a backseat to their work changing perspectives in society. They spent large amounts

CREDIT: Hummel

LEFT: Afghan footballer Khalida Popal plays in defence of human rights

of their time normalising and giving visibility to women playing football.

"I found my purpose in life through football. It helped me to love being a woman in a very male-dominated country," she said. "The voice that I have, the platform, the power and the impact that I'm making through football, just because of football."

She doesn't think she'd have had the same experience through anything other than this particular sport – football allowed her to clearly see challenges around gender. Now, she is the programme director for the Afghan women's national team.

Popal reflects on her childhood. When she kicked a ball around as a schoolgirl, she had to camouflage herself as a boy, wearing baggy clothes and resisting the cheers and shouts that are associated with football, so that her voice wouldn't give her away. Eventually, she was found out. But rather than stopping her in her tracks, this unveiling of her identity spurred her on. With the support of her mother, she set up a girls' club at school in 2002. From there, football for women in Afghanistan took root, with a league in place by 2006 and a national team by 2007.

Whenever she stepped onto a football field, Popal was taking a firm stand against Taliban ideology. She encouraged her teammates to do media interviews, raise their voices and make their faces known.

"They don't want strong women like me," said Popal, a woman in defiance of oppressive gender stereotypes. "They see me as a threat."

When the Taliban first took over in 1996, Popal was very young. She remembers losing access to education, sport and social activities.

"The situation in Afghanistan wasn't ideal, even when the Taliban didn't have full control," she remembered. "The first time the Taliban lost control in Afghanistan, they were still there."

As soon as the group regained full control in the summer of 2021, she knew the women's team would be in serious danger.

"When the country collapsed, of course it was traumatising," she said. "I was grieving for my country. But then I immediately started thinking about all the women who did interviews, all the young women who were very brave who talked publicly about their sexual orientation. Their identities were quite bold and visible."

The time for grieving was over. It was time to take action for the women now banned from playing football.

"How can I help my girls stuck in Afghanistan?" she asked herself.

She spoke to the press, and used her huge football network to find ways to get her squad out, all the time feeling vulnerable as she stepped into the role of leader, potentially putting herself at risk. The former captain used her voice as a tool to lead the evacuation — the squad supporting her behind the scenes was made up of lawyers, coaches and managers.

The women's senior team was evacuated to Australia in early September 2021 and the development team to the UK shortly after. The under-17s team went to Portugal.

But some were left behind and remain there today. The under-15s team is still under threat in the country, forced to stay inside their homes.

"They can't travel. They can't play football. They can't study. They can't do anything," Popal said. She hopes a host country will soon come forward to give them sanctuary.

While most of her fellow footballers might be safe, Popal is disappointed in Fifa. She wants the world's football governing body to allow Afghan women from around the world to come together to represent their country on the global stage by competing in tournaments.

How can I help my girls stuck in Afghanistan?

Inside the country, they are banned from playing football by the Taliban, so those in the diaspora should be given the chance. So far, Fifa has not released a statement.

"The right to represent our country is taken away from the women," Popal said. "They are training, they are practising, but their dreams are taken away."

Her focus on using football for social inclusion has never waned. In 2014, Popal set up Girl Power in Europe and the Middle East, using her own experience to empower refugees and migrants in sport.

"Every girl everywhere should have access to sport, especially to football," she said. "[I hope] that refugees, non-refugees and migrants can also dare to dream. A young girl can dream to play the sport that they'd like to."

Football has been a source of activism for Popal, but she doesn't think that sportspeople should be pressured into action. Activism, she said, should be authentic. Those who want to focus on performance should be allowed to do just that. Others who wish to use their platforms to fight for issues they care about should be kept safe by governing bodies.

Popal left Afghanistan, her loved ones and her dreams to protect her voice. Now it is stronger than ever. She considers her purpose as speaking up for all those women who have lost their own freedom to speak, or who never had that right in the first place.

"To be the voice for them. To stand for them. And stand with them." ✖

Katie Dancey-Downs is assistant editor at Index

51(03):56/57|DOI:10.1177/03064220221126406

Exposing Saudi's nasty tactics

When **ADAM CRAFTON** investigated Saudi Arabia's abuse of LGBTQ+ people following their takeover of Newcastle FC, he too became the subject of abuse. He writes about the experience here

CREDIT: (main) Murad Sezer/Alamy /(right) Saudi Ministry of Commerce

AFTER A MISERABLE 14-year malaise under the ownership of the British retail tycoon Mike Ashley, Premier League football club Newcastle United finally traded hands at the end of 2021. With Ashley at the helm, Newcastle supporters felt the club received little of the necessary investment to compete in the top flight of English football and, as such, the fanbase enthusiastically embraced news of a takeover. The new owners, however, immediately attracted scrutiny

when it emerged that the Saudi Arabian government's sovereign wealth fund, called the Public Investment Fund (PIF), acquired 80% of the club, while their consortium partners PCP Capital and RB Sports Media shared the remaining 20%.

Rapidly, it became the most fiercely-debated takeover in the Premier League era. On the one hand, Amanda Staveley of PCP Capital Partners described PIF as an "autonomous commercially driven investment fund", while the Premier League said in a statement that it had

ABOVE: People attend a funeral prayer for murdered Saudi journalist Jamal Khashoggi at the courtyard of Fatih mosque in Istanbul, Turkey, November 2018

"received legally binding assurances that the Kingdom of Saudi Arabia will not control Newcastle United Football Club."

Yet critics argued that the club's separation from the Saudi state is difficult to take at face value when we consider that, at the time of the takeover, the fund was chaired by Mohammed bin Salman, the Crown Prince and ruler of the kingdom, while PIF's board was composed of six ministers from the Saudi government, as well as a Royal Court advisor. Yasir Al-Rumayyan, the governor of the investment fund who became the chairman of Newcastle, does not have an official governmental position but he is the chair of the state-owned oil business Saudi Aramco. These links became controversial due to the death of Saudi journalist Jamal Khashoggi, who was murdered in the Saudi embassy in Istanbul in 2018 after previously criticising Bin Salman in The Washington Post. According to a US intelligence report, Bin Salman is deemed responsible for approving the operation that killed Khashoggi. Bin Salman describes the findings as flawed and Saudi Arabia has described the findings of the US office of the director of national intelligence as "negative, false and unacceptable".

Beyond the alleged assassination of Khashoggi, reporting of the Newcastle takeover regularly mentioned, often in passing, concerns about the rights and treatment of women and the LGBTQ+ community within Saudi Arabia.

Amnesty International demanded a meeting with the Premier League. They argued the takeover "raises a host of deeply troubling questions about sportswashing, human rights and the integrity of English football".

As a journalist, I was curious as to what exactly it meant to be LGBTQ+ in Saudi Arabia. At The Athletic, a British-US sports publication, we instinctively knew life was difficult for these people. A quick check of any human rights website tells you that Saudi Arabia adheres to strict interpretations of Sharia law, which renders it illegal to be LGBTQ+ and punishable by arrest, lashings, imprisonment or even death.

Our aim was to educate football supporters by humanising the abstract, which meant empowering voices that have been marginalised in Saudi Arabia and providing concrete and

I heard multiple graphic allegations of attempted cure therapy

relatable examples of human rights abuses. The challenge, however, was how to do so when LGBTQ+ Saudis run the risk of retribution by speaking out. In the report, to protect the safety of our numerous interviewees across the LGBTQ+ spectrum, we afforded participants anonymity in order to enable them to speak as freely as possible about their experiences. We also concealed the method of contact, so as to prevent, to the best extent possible, any government agencies from identifying those brave enough to speak out.

The headline of the article on The Athletic laid out their courage: "Risking Death to Tell The Truth". Within the conversations, I heard multiple graphic allegations of attempted cure therapy in some of the country's celebrated "mental health" hospitals, mistreatment by the police, while participants also directed me to the fate of Suhail al-Jameel, a 25-year-old social media influencer reported to have been arrested in 2019 for posting a shirtless picture in leopard-print shorts. Multiple reports claimed that the charge sheet included "cybercrimes", "homosexuality", "imitating a woman", "disobedience" and "public indecency". The Saudi government and embassy in London were contacted for comment but did not respond. PIF, Newcastle United and the Premier League all declined to comment on the record, although sources insisted on the separation between the state and the investment fund.

The gravity of the conversations became clear as, on several occasions, participants raised concerns that I might be a secret member of the Saudi authorities entrapping LGBTQ+ people by moonlighting as a journalist.

Upon releasing the article, the social media impact was significant. My Twitter post sharing the article received three million impressions and over 1,000 retweets. The report received industry acclaim but it also provoked the darkest forces of social media. A Saudi journalist with over 200,000 followers described myself, a gay journalist, as a "petty pervert" who had "started a smear campaign against the Kingdom of Saudi Arabia". He said I "must be flogged". My inbox was soon flooded, by a mixture of death threats, vomit emojis and intimidation. Memes of burning rainbow flags followed and so too did the messages warning that I was destined for hell. Some of these accounts appeared to be bots (the Saudi government has previously been accused of deploying an online troll farm to silence critics) but there also appeared to be an organic response from Saudis who believed I was a Westerner seeking to impose my values on their country.

It was, therefore, a staggering and eye-opening window into the fate of those who amplify the stories that the trolls wish to conceal. It only underlines why such reports remain essential. ✖

Adam Crafton is a reporter at The Athletic

51(03):58/59|DOI:10.1177/03064220221126407

ABOVE: A TV report shows an official removing rainbow-coloured items from shops in Riyadh, Saudi Arabia. It's illegal to be LGBTQ+ in the country and punishments can include death

It's foul play in Kashmir

Amid threats to players and censored documentaries, **BILAL AHMAD PANDOW** charts the influence of the political boot on the Kashmiri football pitch

THE FACE OF Kashmiri football changed in the 1980s, when one player encouraged a whole new generation.

Football was a favourite pastime for young boys in Kashmir – more popular than cricket. Considered a poor man's sport that required only a ball and a field, many professional players from humble families honed their game on the streets without any proper equipment.

One of them was Abdul Majeed Kakroo – the first Kashmiri footballer in India's national team – and he rose to become captain.

"During my childhood days, community friends and I used to play in the middle of the night in Lal Chowk [Red Square] in Srinagar under the streetlights with the least disturbances of automobiles," he told Index. "The main road of Lal Chowk was the field, Ghanta Ghar [the clock tower] was one goalpost and the Palladium Cinema was the other."

The places where Kakroo used to play are at the centre of Kashmir's history. The main field, Lal Chowk, was named after Moscow's Red Square and was an important place for political meetings. The Ghanta Ghar was built →

RIGHT: Boys play football in Srinagar, Jammu and Kashmir

At the peak of militancy during the 1990s, I received threats from militants to quit the Indian team

→ in 1980, and on 26 January 1992, India's Republic Day, Bharatiya Janata Party president Murli Manohar Joshi raised the Indian flag atop the tower, giving it political significance.

That other makeshift goalpost, the Palladium Cinema, is also historically momentous. Once a place to celebrate a love of film, it is now occupied by paramilitary troopers. In 1948, Jawaharlal Nehru, then prime minister of India, stood outside that very cinema and promised a referendum to the people of Jammu and Kashmir to determine their future.

Over the years of conflict, the state conducted football tournaments in an attempt to show normality in the region. Srinagar – the capital of the erstwhile Jammu and Kashmir state, now a union territory – witnessed an unusual summer in 2008 when it hosted the Santosh Trophy, an Indian football tournament which started in 1941.

During a match between Punjab and hosts Jammu and Kashmir, angry local supporters threw stones and shouted anti-India slogans before the game was called off. After a victory against the Delhi team, home fans put up a banner reading "Kashmir defeats India".

But against a backdrop of complicated politics, Kakroo remained apolitical and continued his game.

Along with his fortunes, football rose in the region during the 1970s and 1980s. However, it became increasingly difficult for him to carry on playing for the Indian team.

"At the peak of militancy during the 1990s, I received threats from militants to quit the Indian team. I came back and started playing for a local team in Kashmir and now I am into coaching," Kakroo said.

Meanwhile, Basharat Bashir Baba, another young Kashmiri footballer, was selected for training with Santos Football Club in Brazil.

It was the opportunity of a lifetime, but he was denied travel documents. The issue was Baba's family history – his father had been a militant when Baba was only an infant.

Baba had trained at the International Sports Academy Trust, founded by Juan Marcos Troia, a Fifa-certified coach, and his wife Priscilla to train Kashmiri boys.

He eventually got his passport in 2009, when chief minister of Jammu and Kashmir, Omar Abdullah, intervened after reading about him. But soon after, Indian filmmaker Ashvin Kumar's Inshallah, Football, a documentary of Baba's life, struggled to get released.

The Central Board of Film Certification did not give the film a favourable reception and after a long battle with the censors it was granted an "adult" rating, resulting in severe restrictions on who can see it.

It is a "polite" form of censorship, Kumar told Index at that time. The rating, usually reserved for extreme violence or sexual content, amounted to a de facto ban on the film being broadcast in India.

The film board told Kumar the documentary was too critical of the government. But in spite of the decision, it has since won awards at various international film festivals.

Bilal A. Jan, a filmmaker from Kashmir, told Index that since 2010 when Inshallah, Football was released, the political situation had gone from bad to worse for people in his industry.

Kashmiri filmmakers have attempted to create political and conflict-based films in the past. However, Jan said

they now face security threats and government opposition, adding that while filmmakers from Kashmir had long been self-censoring, now only outsiders can afford to take on such a project as Kumar's.

Back to the pitch, Kakroo told Index about a close shave he had in the mid-1990s. On his way to a practice session at the high-security Bakshi Stadium in Kashmir, which is also used for the Indian Republic Day parade, he was stopped by troopers.

"The security personnel there asked for my identification card," he said. "Had I not carried my ID card that day with me, I don't know what troopers would have done to me."

Over decades of atrocities from both state and militant sides, Kakroo said he had witnessed many cases where footballers were beaten up, threatened and harassed, before giving up the game. In a recent example, from 2020, 21-year-old Amir Siraj, hailing from the north Kashmir town of Sopore, was killed in a gun battle and it was alleged that he was affiliated to a militant group. Another footballer, Majid Khan, from Anantnag in the south, joined a militant group briefly in 2017 but later left following a campaign for him to put down arms.

Recently, private clubs have emerged in the region, but the state has been selective as to which it supports.

The president of the District Football Association in Srinagar, Fayaz Ahmad Sofi, told Index that football should not be dragged into politics.

"The state should support all football clubs and associations equitably, keeping aside the politics and sustaining the game in its true sense," he said.

In Kashmir, the history of football is inseparable from its turbulent political past – a past, it seems, that continues to inform the state of play on the pitch. ✖

Bilal Ahmad Pandow is a researcher and freelance journalist based in Kashmir

51(03):60/62|DOI:10.1177/03064220221126408

How 'industrial football' was used to silence protests

Football fans turned out in large numbers during the Gezi Park protests in Istanbul. They've paid the price since, writes **KAYA GENÇ**

FOOTBALL IS A colossal business in Turkey. The billion-dollar industry constitutes Europe's sixth largest football economy. No wonder the so-called "beautiful game" wields such enormous cultural and political influence on Turks, many of whom define themselves by their loyalty to football clubs Galatasaray, Fenerbahçe and Beşiktaş.

All based in Istanbul, they're known as "the big three", but since the nationalist-Islamist AK Party came to power in 2002, a flurry of other teams, from Trabzonspor to Başakşehir, have risen to prominence, winning national cups and increasingly defining what modern Turkish football is. Unsurprisingly, these teams are government-supported – a prerequisite for any successful business in autocrat President Recep Tayyip Erdoğan's "New Turkey".

Just a decade ago, though, anti-government sentiment defined Turkish football. During the opening ceremony of Galatasaray's fancy new stadium in 2011, Erdoğan greeted fans, expecting gratitude for his role in building the new venue. Instead, boos rose from the terraces.

"It's a key moment in modern AK Party-era Turkish football," said Patrick Keddie, who chronicled the tale of Turkish football in his 2018 book The Passion: Football and the Story of Modern Turkey.

"He expected to be welcomed and thought he would bask in fame, but ended up getting booed... It was around this time that things began to turn. There was this shift from the liberal early-era AK Party to something much more authoritarian and repressive."

Turkish football in those years, Keddie noticed, was "utterly politicised on every level", from activists using the game's national prominence to voice their political anger, to Erdoğan talking up his semi-professional football background for political gain. "There was this mythology of him as a former player."

That 2011 incident, so crushing for an ex-footballer, marked the culmination point of several changes that began in 2002. Acting out of financial self-interest, the government started knocking down stadiums in city centres and replacing them with enormous new ones, subsequently building a dozen more, in the suburbs, in association with Toki, Turkey's public housing body.

Despite such tactics, cronies of the AK Party noticed how impenetrable the "big three" culture remained. Defending the republic's ideals, fans of those teams largely hated the party's oppressive project of Islamist nationalism. So the government began criminalising, imprisoning and demonising dissident fans and managers through a flurry of court cases.

First came the "match-fixing scandal". In the summer of 2011, Erdoğan's prosecutors began investigating football matches they accused of being fixed. On 10 July 2012, a state court ordered the arrest of 61 people. Among the managers and national team players held was Aziz Yıldırım, the strictly secularist president of Fenerbahçe – the club Turkey's founder Mustafa Kemal Atatürk supported and which symbolises his modernising legacy. (A retrial process that began in 2015 cleared Fenerbahçe from all the charges; Yıldırım's case was dropped in 2020.) Week after week, Fenerbahçe fans rushed to courts and, after sentencing, to prisons to show solidarity.

But it was the Beşiktaş fans – particularly the Çarşı group, named after the marketplace where Beşiktaş fans used to gather before matches for a drink – who played a crucial role in 2013's Gezi uprising.

These Istanbul protests started as a movement against the development of the area, but quickly became a focal point of wider anti-government sentiment. Alongside environmentalists, leftists, liberals and other progressive millennials, Beşiktaş fans filled public squares and fought with the police.

Haldun Açıksözlü, an actor and author, wrote two books on Çarşı. "While growing up as a leftist in my youth, my passion for Beşiktaş grew, too," he told Index. "I was part of Çarşı right from its inception."

Rooted in the Ottoman Empire, Turkish football's story begins ➡

Erdoğan expected to be welcomed and thought he would bask in fame, but ended up getting booed

RIGHT: A supporter of Turkish football club Beşiktaş joins in demonstrations at Taksim Square, Istanbul. In June 2013, football fans in Instanbul joined environmentalists, leftists and liberals to fight against government corruption in the Gezi protests

→ with English residents of Salonica introducing the sport to Turks. The first matches were played in 1875. A football league was established in Istanbul in 1904, which soon extended into regional leagues in Anatolian cities and eventually the formation of the nationwide professional league. While Fenerbahçe and Galatasaray were known as teams of the bourgeoise and aristocracy, Beşiktaş was the team of cab drivers and the working classes.

Çarşı fans, Açıksözlü says, are famed for their cosmopolitanism and because they have a vital element of dissent. He said: "The group's founders, from the early 1980s, were all leftists. Çarşı was a fan group that tilted football spectators toward leftist politics in the aftermath of the coup trauma of 12 September 1980. This leftist, communitarian perspective influenced me."

But things turned when Beşiktaş's 70-year-old stadium, İnönü (named after Atatürk's closest ally in founding the republic), was demolished in 2013. "They made a mess of İnönü Stadium in the name of rebuilding it," said Açıksözlü.

Erdoğan, who hates İnönü's secularist politics, ended up excising the name of Turkey's second president from Istanbul with this gesture.

Around this time, "the police and security forces began terrorising Beşiktaş fans", said Açıksözlü. "Perhaps that was why Çarşı played such a prominent role in Gezi. The reaction creates reaction: the unnecessary use of tear gas by the police, their assault on Çarşı fans while they walked on streets with their families – these inevitably pushed Çarşı to the side of the sensitive people of Gezi."

Açıksözlü describes Çarşı's involvement in Gezi as an "incredible tale worthy of movies". It began simply: 50 people walked from Beşiktaş to the nearby Akaretler neighbourhood. Their number grew to 100 at first and then grew to 1,000. When they walked up the hill and reached Gezi Park, the group numbered 2,500. "People heard their chants on the streets and joined in. Anyone who said they wouldn't accept [living] under a one-man regime, wouldn't accept state-intervention in their lives, sided with Çarşı," he said.

Before Gezi, what Keddie – the British journalist – knew about Turkish football was clichéd: that it had crazy fans, that the big three Istanbul clubs hated each other. "I was surprised to see how prominent those fans were in the protests," Keddie said. "They were on the forefront, fighting the police, manning the barricades."

Still, the "big three" culture proved hard to penetrate for Keddie, who struggled with mingling with fans. "I think they're insular and clannish and suspicious of outsiders – especially journalists."

→

Turkish football in those years was 'utterly politicised on every level'

→ By the time Beşiktaş opened its new stadium on 10 April 2016, Keddie had noticed that Turkey's political equation had changed dramatically. On the opening day, when Erdoğan sprinted and kicked a ball on the pitch, the stands were free of spectators. Even if they wanted to, nobody could boo him now.

When he visited the new stadium, Açıksözlü saw "airplane seats with special monitors attached to them", and decided the old spirit of Çarşı was gone.

"There was this period, from 2011 to 2014, when the protest movement was quite intense," Keddie said, "but by April 2016, most of the protests had died down or got more subtle for various reasons. Turkey didn't have these major events, these major triggers, anymore. The biggest recent scandal of European football, the match-fixing case, 2013's massive Gezi Park protests, and its aftermath – all of that had faded. With some exceptions, all forms of protest were essentially banned in Turkey."

A significant factor behind the demise of Turkey's protest culture was Passolig, an electronic ticket system the government introduced in 2014. "The electronic fan card Passolig was introduced as part of the country's efforts to tackle hooliganism and violence in football," announced the AK Party-run Anadolu Agency. "The new practice aims at a better identification of fans involved in violence in stadiums."

In reality, Passolig was a cunningly conceived mechanism to detain dissident football fans. "Bringing in the Passolig card cowed many fans, and it made them think twice about protesting and even chanting because that system came with a whole load of security protocol and surveillance systems," said Keddie.

It was much easier to identify anti-government protesters, ban them from stadiums and even charge and imprison them. "It was a response, the authorities said, to hooliganism and disorder, but most fans considered it a way to control them politically. It also gentrified the sport, making it more manageable, more middle class."

Açıksözlü pointed to the formation of the 1453 group, a nationalist fans' group, as another form of secret state intervention. "Specially assigned people were sent to Galatasaray's Aslan Pençesi fan group and the Tek Yumruk group of Fenerbahçe. Their job was to stop fans looking at events from a leftist perspective."

Anger soon melted into silence. Concern for security triumphed. Today, most fans wonder why they should risk their safety under an oppressive regime: Erdoğan sued more than 38,000 Turks for defamation between 2015 and 2021. Besides, for many devoted fans, it's costly to go to matches at big clubs now. After Beşiktaş relocated, Çarşı had a much less prominent place in the new stadium. And outside the glossy new venues, Keddie observed, "the police are deployed in heavy numbers and they are happy to use violence whenever they need to".

Açıksözlü said "industrial football" had destroyed the pleasures of the game. "Did you hear anything about Çarşı in the past five years? Did you read anything about other fan groups? Because of Passolig, the fan groups no longer influence Turkish football."

Still, the protest culture lives on, despite going underground. Fans can still be heard chanting about Atatürk, and when they sing the famed Izmir March, with lyrics including "Long live Atatürk! Your name will be written on a precious stone", it's a message directed at the Islamists.

Opposition politicians are playing ball, too. After a match between Galatasaray and the government-funded Başakşehir ended 2-0, the leader of the İYı Party, Meral Akşener, tweeted: "Galatasaray 2 – Erdoğan 0." Many in Turkey call Başakşehir "Erdoğanspor".

When another member of the opposition, Ekrem İmamoğlu, won Istanbul's mayoral elections in 2019 but was refused the mandate after Erdoğan accused him of being a "terrorist", a "liar" and a "thief", the young politician, an ex-goalkeeper, visited football stadiums for support.

"Football is a big part of İmamoğlu's brand," Keddie said. "He was a goalie in his youth. So after the election was cancelled, he went to stadiums of the big three, pointedly avoiding smaller clubs, especially Başakşehir. Fans at those stadiums were chanting, 'Give him the mandate'." Once he was re-elected as mayor, İmamoğlu pledged to defend the interests of the big three.

Meanwhile, the "artificial success" of Başakşehir, Keddie said, may prove temporary. "I don't see Başakşehir as really having power because they're not an authentic, grassroots project. They don't have many fans... It's like a top-down project team; after all those years of investment and success in winning the league, they still get terrible attendances. It's a cultural thing. Every other team sneers at them. Even people who support the government and support Beşiktaş or Galatasaray sneer at them."

The AK Party may play dirty again, reject the results of next year's presidential elections and invite their hardline supporters to the streets to terrorise people. But then Turkey's oppressed football fans can make a return, too, and protect Atatürk's legacy.

"I spoke to a lot of people from Çarşı," Keddie recalled, "and they said: 'Yes, we're against the government, and if something like Gezi happened again, we'd be there in a heartbeat.'" ✖

Kaya Genç is Index's contributing editor for Turkey. He is based in Istanbul

51(03):63/66|DOI:10.1177/03064220221126410

Xi's real China dream

China's leader is football mad and he has put the sport at the forefront of many initiatives. When it comes to the nation's freedoms that's been a mixed blessing, writes **JONATHAN SULLIVAN**

THE NEAR COINCIDENCE of two events this autumn – the World Cup in Qatar and the 20th National Party Congress in Beijing, where Chinese leader Xi Jinping will likely assume an unprecedented third term in power – represents an appropriate moment to reflect on one of Xi's signature initiatives. Not the Chinese Dream, the Belt and Road Initiative, poverty alleviation or his anti-corruption campaign, but football.

Legend holds that a soccer-mad young Xi was so aggrieved by the "humiliation" inflicted on the Chinese national team by English club Watford at an exhibition game he attended at the Workers' Stadium in 1983 that he determined he would redress China's weakness in football. Decades later he declared, shortly before assuming power, that China would host and ultimately win the World Cup.

As a means to overcoming the country's historical "national humiliation", it was probably overly ambitious.

Nonetheless, in his first term Xi put football reform and development squarely on the national political agenda through three major policy documents promulgated between 2014 and 2016. Together they represented an overarching framework for developing a domestic sports economy, facilitating mass participation and creating an effective training ecosystem from youth levels to the national team. The long-term objective was to transform China into a "world class football nation" by 2050, a timeframe and scale of ambition that aligned with broader national objectives such as the "great rejuvenation of the Chinese nation".

Common to Chinese policymaking, broad top-down objectives were delegated to many different institutional and private actors to design and implement, leading to much experimentation, messy ad hoc adjustment and competing interests.

Compared with many other initiatives associated with Xi's tenure, football is a benign sector. Many concerns raised at the height of the football craze a few years ago have, as yet, proven unfounded. Chinese companies' global sponsorship deals and the elevation of Chinese officials within international governance bodies have not made the global game any more corrupt or susceptible to parochial interests.

Chinese investors' rush to demonstrate fealty to Xi's football plans (or merely to secrete money offshore) led to a brief, and now largely divested, scattergun acquisition of European football clubs and assets, but the clubs and leagues survived and even though many were in globally strategic locations it did not result in additional "geopolitical influence". Nor did the funding and construction of stadiums in Africa, though there may have been marginal "soft power" gains in facilitating the hosting of several Africa Cup of Nations tournaments.

Imposing Xi's favourite sport across Chinese school curricula might appear heavy handed, but encouraging China's sedentary youth to exercise and head

off a public health timebomb is hardly a pernicious objective.

Football is Xi's pet project, but criticism of the underperforming national team, the hapless Chinese Football Association (CFA) or broader reforms are subject to no more stringent censorship than anything else on the Chinese internet (contained criticism is OK, demands for systemic change or encouraging collective action is not).

It is true that Chinese football reproduces class and place-based disparities, with migrant workers, for example, less able to participate. And, prior to Covid, match-going fans were already facing increasingly strict security at stadiums, fickle owners and idiosyncratic regulatory interventions by the CFA. And yet while we should be mindful of the progressive circumscription of freedoms across Chinese society under Xi, many of the problems faced by Chinese fans are common to supporters everywhere.

That said, we should pause for a moment on the question of ethnicity, given the unprecedented crackdown on Muslims in Xinjiang that has come to define Xi's 10 years in office. On the surface, football has become a site for advances in representation. China's best player, Wu Lei, is a member of the Hui (Muslim) ethnic minority group. In March, Chinese-Nigerian Huang Shenghao became the first bi-racial player to represent the country (at under-17 level). Mirahmetjan Muzepper became the first Uyghur to play for the men's national team in 2018.

The treatment of another Uyghur player, Erfan Hezim, demonstrates the systemic repression of young Uyghur men. Hezim spent almost a year in a detention camp in Xinjiang, apparently for unauthorised travel overseas to participate in football training camps, →

≡ Football schools and academies have not (yet) produced a "Chinese Messi"

➜ before being allowed to resume his career in 2019. Uyghurs coming through the ranks can face many forms of discrimination, partly explaining the negligible number of players in the Chinese Super League despite the popularity of football in Xinjiang. The region could be a significant source of playing talent, but the conditions there are so severely circumscribed that it is impossible to realise.

As for those from outside China's official borders, the expedient decision to bring several naturalised Brazilians into the national team during World Cup qualifying met with only muted criticism from grassroot nationalists, even after the players' efforts proved futile. The handling of naturalised talent, though, demonstrates an enduringly awkward official embrace of foreignness. The CFA's provisional regulations oblige clubs to teach naturalised foreigners Chinese language, culture and history, in addition to the fundamental political positions of the CCP. Party cadres attached to every professional club monitor, supervise and submit regular reports on players' performance, behaviour and attitudes, reproducing the party's longstanding "foreign affairs" system for handling foreigners. By all accounts, the naturalised Brazilians have been exemplary. But all this shows that some aspects of football's development

BELOW: College students play football in Harbin, China, as President Xi Jinping envisions China becoming a world class football nation by 2050

reflect the trajectory emerging across other social sectors during Xi's tenure – one of a controlled society subject to the regime's circumscriptions and vision for a desirable China.

In line with the requirements of the reform policies, infrastructure has been built and facilities rolled out on an impressive scale. But football has so far failed to become an elective mass participation sport like basketball or badminton. The popularity of gaming and the exponential growth of

professional e-sports in China suggests football has its work cut out appealing to young people.

China has its fair share of dedicated supporters and "transnational fans" who are as knowledgeable and passionate about foreign clubs they will never visit as locals are. Yet the kind of intangible "football culture" that manifests in ubiquitous pick-up games on Brazilian beaches or English playgrounds has not taken root. Football schools and academies have not (yet) produced a "Chinese Messi" or even a supply of more prosaic talent, although it is premature to write off long-term efforts to build up the talent pool.

Youth participation has run afoul of resistant parents who prefer their children to focus on academics, which is intense, uber-competitive and almost certainly a better investment in the future than football. Short fee-paying football camps are the preserve of cosmopolitan middle-class parents, while serious football academies offering talent-based scholarships are mainly an option for poor families whose children are unable to compete for academic advancement. Football as a leisure activity and signifier of middle-class lifestyles embodying China's desired "mildly prosperous" modernity has so far failed to capture imaginations.

And then came Covid and continuing "dynamic zero" restrictions to burst football's bubble economy. With the Chinese Super League (CSL) mothballed for a time, expensively-acquired foreign players departed, and China gave up its hosting rights for the 2023 Asian Cup due to the ongoing uncertainties. Owners facing economic headwinds created by the pandemic were unable to service the continual cash injections needed to sustain clubs.

The property sector, which has become intimately entwined with football, was hit by a debt crisis and state interventions associated with Xi's new preoccupation of 'Common Prosperity'. Evergrande, the

over-leveraged real-estate developer and owner of China's most successful club, was forced to sell the land for its half-built new mega-stadium back to the local government. Since 2015, more than 20 clubs across the top divisions have folded, often due to insufficient organisational experience and unsustainable business models. Jiangsu FC disbanded soon after winning the CSL in 2020 when its owner, indebted retailer Suning, decided it could no longer afford it.

There is no reason why Chinese football shouldn't find a sustainable niche as a spectator and participant sport, and a national team that can compete in Asia and qualify for international tournaments. Some of the ambitions set out in Xi's reforms are not currently realistic, but long-term plans should be given time to unfold. A hypothetical Chinese bid to host a future World Cup, would, given Fifa's interests and track record, prove irresistible. The hosting of a World Cup would be a significant boost to football development in the country. But the attendant potential for "sportswashing" and requisite self-censorship have already been demonstrated on a small scale by European clubs and leagues desperate to access the Chinese market. Take the example of midfielder Mesut Özil, who was sidelined by Arsenal, which has a huge following in China, after speaking out against the persecution of Uyghurs.

The Chinese national team will not compete in Qatar later this year, but China will be present through Fifa's signature sponsorship deal with Wanda, and Chinese fans will watch en masse, attracted by the spectacle, the conversation and the opportunities for offshore sports-betting. ✖

Jonathan Sullivan is a Chinese specialist and an associate professor at the University of Nottingham

51(03):67/69|DOI:10.1177/03064220221126411

CREDIT: Ronen Zvulun/Alamy

Tackling Israel's thorny politics

Bnei Sakhnin, Israel's top Arab football team, offers a rare opportunity for Arabs to voice their support of Palestine. Still, that comes at a cost, writes **DANIELLA PELED**

FOR SOME, IT'S a heart-warming tale of how a minor team from a small city in the Galilee, northern Israel, with a population of just over 30,000, fought to a historic victory in the State Cup in 2004. It's a symbol of co-existence, with an Arab-majority team directed by a Jewish manager becoming the first team of its kind to play in what was then the Uefa Cup.

But for the Palestinian citizens of Israel, who make up just over 20% of the country's population, it's their de facto national team. In mainstream Israeli society, there is very little room for this kind of expression of alternative identity. This means that Sakhnin's top players can be national heroes who are reviled for not fully embracing Zionism, while their fans are viewed as traitors for flying Palestinian flags at the same time as watching a largely state-funded team.

"Sakhnin is a lot of different things to a lot of different people," said Bassil Mikdadi, who runs a popular blog about football in Palestine. The change in the team's fortunes over the past 20 or so years, he explained, has been accompanied by a drastic shift to the right in wider Israeli society.

Bnei Sakhnin /Abna Sakhnin (Sons of Sakhnin in Hebrew and Arabic respectively) started off in the 1960s as a small-town team, bumbling along with little financial backing and few achievements until a 1991 merger with another local team boosted its fortunes. It reached the country's second tier in 1997, but ran into problems when its stadium was shut on security grounds, leading to a significant financial cost and the loss of the home side's advantage.

LEFT: Fans of Arab-majority team Bnei Sakhnin arrive to watch a match against Beitar Jerusalem, a team notorious for its right-wing racist fans, at Teddy Stadium in Jerusalem

"One can say this was a political decision," explained writer Nicholas Blincoe, author of More Noble Than War: The Story of Football in Israel and Palestine. He noted that the man responsible, regional police commander Guy Reif, was later dismissed after firing a gun at his own offices in an apparent attempt to justify his insistence that he was in the midst of an Arab terrorist conspiracy.

"The minute Reif was sacked they started playing at home again – there were no security risks – and that's what helped them improve radically," Blincoe said. That said, the stadium has been periodically shut since, including late last year, but perhaps with more basis. Public safety concerns continue, especially over policing matches with fierce rivals such as Beitar Jerusalem, notorious for its ultra-right wing following.

As soon as they entered the Premier League in 2003, Sakhnin appointed a Jewish manager and signed two Jewish players. In 2004, to national incredulity and delight, they won the State Cup – the Israeli equivalent of the English FA Cup. Sakhnin's win came during a particularly dark period for the country, emerging from the ravages of the second intifada.

"It was an incredibly unhappy time, with few bright spots," Blincoe said. "Sakhnin's victory seemed to show what the future might hold."

At the time, club chairman Mazen Ghnaim said: "We have qualified for Europe and we will prove to the world how to make peace between Jews and Arabs."

But the faultlines stubbornly remained. "Football is definitely the national sport of Israel, the most popular and the one that draws in the biggest crowds," said Ben Sharoni, a sports writer for the liberal Israeli Haaretz newspaper. "Even though Israel has more achievements in basketball, an international football match is always a major event," Sharoni added.

This meant that when Arabic captain Abbas Suan scored the equalising goal in the last minute of the World Cup qualifier against Ireland in 2006, it made him a national hero. But earlier, during the national anthem – Hatikvah (The Hope), which is all about the yearning of a Jewish soul for its homeland – he and Walid Badir, the Israeli team's other Arab player, gazed at the ground rather than singing.

This kind of behaviour is anathema to most Jewish Israelis, who also see Sakhnin's fans' clear identification with Palestine as a straightforward provocation. Supporters fly Palestinian flags in the stands and wave banners featuring symbols such as Handala, the iconic cartoon image of a barefoot boy with his back turned towards the viewer, representing Palestinian resistance. Songs can be nationalistic, with bursts of the classic protest chant "With our spirit, with our blood, we'll sacrifice ourselves for al-Aqsa [Jerusalem]."

"Making a distinction between Israeli Arabs and Palestinians is important for a lot of Israeli Jews," Sharoni said. "If there was a scale of racism, the Palestinians would be at the bottom, then Israeli Arabs, then other minorities, and then white Jewish Israelis at the top."

All of this is thrown into particularly sharp relief by the flamboyant extremism of fans of Israel's largest football club, Beitar Jerusalem – the only club in Israel never to have included Arab players. So pronounced is the racism within Beitar that the club's new owner, Moshe Hogeg, said he would tackle its racist image as a priority. Whether that will happen is yet to be seen.

"When Sakhnin play Beitar, [supporters'] coaches have to have a police accompaniment," noted Blincoe. "There have always been problems... Racism and bigotry bleeds into [football]."

As Jewish Israelis shifted to the right, Mikdadi said that Palestinians began to

Supporters fly Palestinian flags in the stands and wave banners featuring symbols such as Handala

consolidate into a more unified identity, with the distinction between those in the West Bank and Gaza (who live under Israeli military occupation) and within Israel itself (where they have full citizenship) increasingly redundant.

"Historically, Israel's hope was to depoliticise the Arabs, to think of themselves as citizens of the state, concerned with the cost of living - not very political, like in any other developed country," he said. "For the multitude, this failed."

The nail in the coffin, he said, was the passing of the 2018 Nation State Law, which delegated Arabic from a state language to one of "special status" and made clear that the right of national self-determination applied only to Jewish citizens. Then came the May 2021 violence in Gaza, which sparked unprecedented Palestinian anger within Israel.

The deepening faultlines in self-expression, heritage and belonging have been reflected on the pitch as much as anywhere else in society.

"I don't think that 15 years ago it would be that common to see Palestinian flags in grounds," Mikdadi said. "If people call you a 'dirty Arab' then at some point they will say, 'OK, I am Arab and this is my flag. Why are we suppressing our national identity?'" ✖

Daniella Peled is managing editor at the Institute for War and Peace Reporting

51(03):70/71|DOI:10.1177/03064220221126412

The stench of white elephants

JAMIL CHADE exposed the corruption surrounding Brazil's hosting of the World Cup. Here he says why the great sporting event was a poisoned chalice

I N GREEK MYTHOLOGY, the gods' intentions to destroy a village were preceded by an orgy organised for those who, later, would discover they would perish. It was an unprecedented feast that would last for days with wine, music and dancing. In Brazil, recent history chimes with mythology.

In 2023, the country will mark 10 years since the first of the mega sporting events was hosted in the country and, with it, an unexpected turnaround in the country's destiny.

In 2013, Brazil hosted the Fifa Confederations Cup, an event that would serve as a rehearsal for the World Cup in 2014. Two years later, it would be the Olympics hosted by the Cariocas (as people in Rio de Janeiro are known). The sequence of events caused envy around the world, while many claimed the Brazilian Decade could catapult the nation into a new level of development.

But these events led to seismic shifts in Brazilian politics and society – shifts that are still being very much felt today.

For the government, the tournaments would be used as a shortcut for the country to become a protagonist on the world stage, confirming a transformation in its foreign policy and the desire to sit at the table with the big powers. For mayors, governors and many other authorities operating at a local level, they would be a political springboard as well as a financial one.

But the events were marked by the corruption of values, resources and democracy itself.

The extreme right used their mismanagement as an opportunity to begin a process of questioning the entire power structure and, thus, pave the way to overthrow those who were in charge.

Media freedom started to suffer from

> It was clear that the organisers had no plan to use the games to ensure a sustainable future

CREDIT: Brazil Photos/Alamy

the get-go. Uncovering corruption in sports meant challenges for me and my fellow journalists.

ABOVE: Demonstration in Rio de Janeiro against the hosting of the 2014 Fifa World Cup in Brazil, June 2013

Media professionals who would "play the game" with the organisers of the Olympic Games or the World Cup had access to the sports stars. They'd be able to line up exclusive interviews and would be rewarded, either with a scoop or other favours.

On the flipside, those opting to question and fulfil their duties as journalists were barred from certain places, ignored by the media department and bullied and discredited by the event organisers.

With an army of legal advisers, sports officials would not hesitate to engage in "lawfare" in order to block a story from being published.

Initially, the Brazilian Football Confederation had promised it would not ask for a single cent of public money to erect the new stadiums the country would need for the World Cup. Less than a decade later, of every $9 spent on the event, $8 had been borrowed, donated or financed by taxpayers.

There was an explosion in construction costs and it was clear the organisers had no plan to use the games in a sustainable way, neither for the cities that hosted them nor for the development of a competitive sports culture. Months after the World Cup final, the lack of games at the Mané Garrincha stadium in Brasília obliged the government to transfer part of its bureaucracy to the stadium, using the rooms for various departments. The outside area was turned into a garage for city buses. It was a similar fate for many of the other stadiums built for the tournament. The World Cup in Brazil became an extravagant mirror of an illusion, and the white elephants and their stench became monuments of a failed adventure.

Two years later, the Olympics in Rio were another tribute to obscenity. Months after the Olympic circus closed, the state of Rio de Janeiro showed clear evidence that it was bankrupt. Pensions started to be taxed, social programmes were cut and salary increases were cancelled. The national economy entered its worst recession, with unemployment affecting 13 million people.

As politicians and businessmen were put in jail for corruption and the economy was ruined, a statement by International Olympic Committee president Thomas Bach at the closing ceremony in Rio still resonates in the country. According to him, holding

The events were marked by the corruption of values, resources and democracy itself

the Games in such a difficult political climate was a "miracle". A miracle for whom, one could ask.

The chaos, however, was not limited to financial collapse or corruption scandals. In 2013, in the midst of the protests, the seeds of the extreme right were planted. While millions of Brazilians took to the streets to demand that the funds for the World Cup be allocated to health and education, far-right groups infiltrated these demonstrations and they turned violent. Posters calling for the return of the military dictatorship were a sign that public fury was being kidnapped.

Authoritarian radicalism took a new dimension, benefiting from a political vacuum and an orchestrated parliamentary coup against then-president Dilma Rousseff, who was impeached in 2016. It was all covered up by the cloak of the need to fight corruption.

Less than five years later, the far right won the 2018 election. Jair Bolsonaro rose to power and immediately implemented his project to dismantle democracy. Ten years after Brazil started hosting the most coveted sporting events on the planet, the ground continues to shake in the country. Not because of the celebration of a goal or a medal but due to the political and social earthquakes they triggered. ✖

Jamil Chade is an award-winning columnist from Brazil

51(03):72/73|DOI:10.1177/0306422022126436

The real game is politics

Some players in Kenya had hopes that football could unite a dissatisfied population. But corruption has meant the national team is suspended from international matches by Fifa. **ISSA SIKITI DA SILVA** reports from Nairobi

ABOVE: Charity sports projects in Kenya aim to bring children together through football. In this case in Kibera, Nairobi

CREDIT: George Philipas/Alamy

A TRUCK CARRYING SUPPORTERS cheering for their political candidate stops near a depleted, gravelly football pitch in Umoja Innercore, an area on the outskirts of the Kenyan capital Nairobi. The atmosphere is festive as loudspeakers pump out songs praising the candidate and party hardliners distribute caps and T-shirts emblazoned with the politician's face.

Youths pushing rickshaws full of water containers to sell to residents whose taps ran dry more than a decade ago launch a barrage of insults towards the convoy, which is trying to capture the attention of the players on the pitch in the futile hope of making them vote.

But on this football pitch it is business as usual, as young people largely ignore the political landscape.

This scene took place in the weeks leading up to the election in August and most players gathered said they were no longer interested in voting, either for the opposition or for the ruling party, as previous elections did not seem to improve their lives.

"We only count when there is an election," one of them, who gave his name as Fundi, told Index.

"Then you see them going street to street, singing and talking nonsense and lies to canvass for votes. Once they are elected they forget us and life goes on, without hope for the future."

Fundi would like to see the nation's youth interested in politics and hopes that they can bond over politics as they bond on the pitch. He said: "I think it is high time we, as committed footballers, start looking for peaceful ways of protesting against the way this country is being run."

Fundi suggested rallying more senior players and mobilising supporters before boycotting matches and hoisting banners that stand up against police brutality, the teargassing of protesters and harassment of journalists.

"It will raise international awareness about the problems our country is facing and will force politicians to wake up from their slumber," he said.

Fundi is not the only one trying to use the pitch to improve the country. In Kibera, another suburb of Nairobi which has been known for violence around elections, the residents partnered with County Governance Watch, a Kenyan non-profit that encourages civic participation, to organise a football match.

"Soccer matters today because it has brought together players who come from different worlds and different villages," said Owino Kotieno, who helped organise the tournament.

In an interview with Al Jazeera, he explained that the game brought together people from different backgrounds who supported different candidates, all united through playing together.

But the game was to no avail. Weeks later, Kenyans headed to the polls in an election that had low voter turnout, and Deputy President William Ruto was declared the winner amid an outcry that the election was rigged.

Dissatisfaction towards politics in Kenya has been rising in recent years. Scores of unemployed, poor youths long for justice, equality, freedom of expression, freedom of assembly and the end of corruption and police brutality. Many describe politicians as thieves in suits, but they're disillusioned and don't know where to turn.

In the lead-up to Ruto's "win", chaos erupted from protesters who believed the election was corrupt. The police responded with tear gas. It is not the first time protests have ended in violence.

Not far from the Umoja football ground, police had shot dead two men during the Covid-19 lockdown.

"Every time we try to protest against these senseless and endless killings by the police, we are teargassed and some of us get arrested. The voice of the youth of this country is not being heard by the authorities," Njoro, a goalkeeper, said.

While some believe football could be used as a powerful tool to help in the battle against corruption in the country, others are less convinced. A sports administrator, on condition of anonymity, told Index that footballers must concentrate on playing football and stay out of politics.

"We will not tolerate that our stadiums and pitches be used as a battleground for political ideas or to incite hatred against the government," he said.

"The players are paid to play football, entertain the masses and represent their country at the highest level if the opportunity arises. These are the rules of Fifa, not mine or anyone else at Football Kenya Federation."

"If they want to make their voices heard or enter politics, they should hang up their boots and join a political party."

Football has been used politically for all the wrong reasons. Military history writer Anthony Clayton says that in Kenya football was initially introduced by the colonialists in urban areas and elite schools and was used as a tool of segregation and social control.

The current leadership continues to use football, in this case as a weapon of forging a false sense of national unity and trying to maintain peace amid election turmoil. Analysts feared the election would lead to violence – and they were right.

Football in this east African nation of 53.8 million seems to be lying on its deathbed, as Kenya has been suspended from international football by Fifa for political interference. The suspension has soured the joy of millions of fans who thought they would be cheering on their national team at the African Cup of Nations 2023 if they qualified.

And bad governance has put a dent in the lives of thousands of footballers who pinned their hopes on this sport to make a living in this unequal society, infested by rampant corruption and nepotism, police brutality, tribalism and numerous incidents of violations of fundamental freedoms.

There is an irony, though. Precisely because Kenyan football has become corrupt, players often come together to discuss this. And that leads to discussions on politics more generally.

A group of footballers, coaches and supporters gathered on a bumpy ground, amid freezing temperatures in Mathare, an impoverished area of Nairobi, after a training session to do just that.

"Football in this country is going nowhere – and if it is the case, ➔

They should hang up their boots and join a political party

➔ then our lives are also coming to a standstill because this is our only hope to make a living," a man named Okello told the crowd.

Another, a Gor Mahia FC supporter named Sonny, said: "I think it's time for us to stand up as one man and fight for our rights. After all, we are the ones disbursing our hard-earned cash to buy tickets to watch the games."

In August last year, fans of Gor Mahia FC and AFC Leopards, two of Kenya's most illustrious clubs, held demonstrations in Nairobi to protest against the 10 million Kenyan shilling

....

BELOW: William Ruto addresses supporters at a campaign rally ahead of the August general election, which he won amid cries of foul play

Once they are elected they forget us and life goes on, without hope for the future

($84,000) fine imposed on their teams by the FKF. The fans paraded their banners at the National Archives as they sang their teams' theme songs in protest of the fines, local media reports said – adding that they threatened to storm the soccer body's offices.

"That, we did for our team," said Sonny. "This time it's going to be for a national cause to demand the end of corruption and bad governance, and justice for all the victims of police brutality, the dead and those who are facing life-threatening injuries."

Another player, Joseph, told Index

that football in Kenya could not be dissociated from politics.

"You'll be killing history," he said. "The soccer fans' revolution is gathering momentum. It will soon deliver."

Football hasn't delivered soon enough. Ruto is now firmly in power and discontent is sky high. But there is always another game, and – it is hoped – another election. ✖

Issa Sikiti da Silva is an Index contributing editor based in west Africa

....

51(03):74/76|DOI:10.1177/03064220221126437

COMMENT

"I saw myself through sport. Any challenges I have ever faced in my life I can find an analogy within football"

PERMI JHOOTI | THE OTHER HALF, P.80

Refereeing rights

Do sports stars have a duty to be politically active? **JULIAN BAGGINI** argues that the responsibility lies elsewhere

ABOVE: Everton players kneel in support of Black Lives Matter ahead of a Premier League match in 2021, while Brentford striker Ivan Toney stands. Toney has said he believes players are being "used as puppets" when they kneel down

T IS INCREASINGLY uncomfortable to be a politically engaged sports fan. As big sport has become big business, more and more international events are moving to countries that have highly questionable human rights records.

I'm sure I'm not the only one whose usual enthusiasm for the men's football World Cup was tempered by Russia's hosting in 2018, or who felt unmotivated tuning into the 2022 Winter Olympics in Beijing following China's recent actions in Xinjiang and Hong Kong.

In motor racing, Formula One's willingness to follow the money means the race calendar includes a grand tour of wealthy but corrupt regimes.

Qatar's hosting of the 2022 men's football World Cup is just another sign of how sport has prioritised money over fair play off the field. Amnesty has highlighted the country's human rights abuses of migrant workers, women and LGBTQ+ people, as well as its lamentable freedom of expression. The successful bid to host the tournament has been plagued by accusations of corruption, which – although unproven

> Speaking out may come at less cost but they may still fear damaging their careers

– seem to many observers to be strong.

Fans can easily choose to tune out or vent their objections. But what about the players? Should they be refusing to play, or at least making some kind of public protest?

In one sense, the answer is obviously yes. Anyone who participates in an event that helps give credibility and income to a corrupt regime becomes complicit. That does not mean it is always wrong to engage, but it does mean there are negative consequences which ought to be counteracted.

The most straightforward way of doing this is to counter the positive PR by speaking out. There's a strong case that this is done more effectively by participating than not. Imagine, for instance, that one of the world's best players, such as Argentina's Lionel Messi or Poland's Robert Lewandowski, refused to play in Qatar. That would put its human rights record in the global spotlight for a day or two. But if they went to the tournament and spoke out while they were there, the impact could be greater, and it would be more likely to get through to Qataris.

However, while we should rightly applaud any player who refuses to just kick the ball and shut up, I'm less convinced that we could reasonably expect them to do so. There is an important difference between actions which are morally required and others which are "supererogatory", meaning they are laudable but optional.

But like most binaries, it is more helpful to think of a sliding scale. While some actions are absolutely required and others obviously optional, in between there are degrees of obligation. My contention is that the obligation for footballers to speak out or opt out on Qatar is weak, because we cannot reasonably expect them to be able and willing to take the most admirable moral stance.

First, think about what refusing to participate would mean for them. Professional footballers have short careers so they could be depriving themselves of the peak of their professional lives. Speaking out may come at less cost but they may still fear damaging their careers. Because the cost of action could be quite high, the obligation to take it has to be commensurably lower.

These are young men who travel the world and know enough to be aware that moral norms vary between nations. But should we expect them to be able to make carefully calibrated decisions about which countries are beyond the pale? It is easy to imagine them thinking, "Qatar may not be perfect, but compared with what the UK and the USA did in Iraq and Afghanistan, its crimes are minor." That's not a very sophisticated moral argument, of course, but many intellectuals defend more complex versions.

A player's failure to reach the best all-things-considered judgement is no more blameworthy than the morally sub-optimal choices most "ordinary" people make. Many people buy meat and dairy sourced from animals kept in terrible conditions, goods made by Uyghurs in internment camps, go on holiday in countries with bad human rights records. When we say they shouldn't do all these things, we are right. But we don't judge them too harshly for doing so because we know that once you start thinking about what is ethical or not, it gets very complicated very quickly, and it is difficult to see the seriousness of an issue when the rest of society is behaving as though nothing is amiss.

There is also a risk that if we pressure players into speaking out and taking action on moral and political issues, we could actually end up with many choosing the wrong causes. Asking young, unintellectual, rich people to take on the role of society's moral spokespeople is giving them a task they are ill-equipped to carry out.

In sport, the main responsibility for ensuring that regimes do not use "sportswashing" to gloss over their human rights abuses lies with those higher up the power command – people who are generally older, more experienced and with a better grasp of the wider situation. Fifa, world football's governing body, should take into account the human rights situation in a country before awarding it a major tournament to host. National governing bodies should take clear public stands and ensure that if their teams are required to play in disreputable countries, there is no complicity with breaches of human rights. Team managers should be charged with communicating such views to the wider public.

The idea that sports people should be role models is overplayed. They should model good qualities such as fair play, dedication, teamwork and respect for opponents because those are the qualities that they can reasonably be expected to have. But to ask them to model statesmanship and political activism is like asking our elected politicians to be exemplars of good exercise regimes or artistic creativity. ✖

Julian Baggini is a writer and the academic director of the Royal Institute of Philosophy

> While we should rightly applaud any player who refuses to just kick the ball and shut up, I'm less convinced that we could reasonably expect them to do so

51(03):78/79|DOI:10.1177/03064220221126441

The other half

PERMI JHOOTI's story inspired the hit film Bend It like Beckham. Here she writes about how football allowed her to express herself, to a point

AM THE FIRST British Asian professional footballer in the UK. A member of the first women's Professional Football team.

Yes. But.

Let me tell you about that move. The ball is played through defence. I am running past them all. It is just me, the goalkeeper, the ball. At full speed, throwing myself through the air. I connect first and the goalkeeper, sliding down, just a fraction too late, watches the ball fly over her.

That moment. That magical 100% moment. The whole of me alive, in motion, committed. Has there ever been a moment in my 'off pitch' life in which I had to give so much of myself?

If you had waited two more hours before calling the ambulance, she would have died.

The move that nearly ended it all. My foot had got to the ball first. The goalkeeper's feet had no ball left to connect to, they drove straight into my stomach.

Cried out. Didn't cry. Unlucky timing.

I didn't even score. The ball floated just over the bar. I never wanted to play football ever again.

The End.

Yes. But.

Let me tell you about that move. The ball is played through defence. I am running past them all. It is just me, the goalkeeper, the ball. At full speed,

throwing myself through the air. I connect first and the goalkeeper, sliding down just a fraction too late, watches the ball fly over her.

Crying. Only crying. Perfect timing.

The move that started it all. My foot got to the ball first. It sailed over the goalkeeper into the net.

Fulham were about to form the first professional women's team. I was playing in my comeback match after That Move Part 1. Nine months between them. A new life. A new beginning.

A professional footballer! What a dream that must be!

Yes. But.

They don't see me. You don't see me!

My constant cry as a child. I don't know who I was screaming at. My parents? Teachers? Those around me? Or myself.

How do I know if you see me or not, when I don't understand myself, haven't had the opportunity to look. Who will hold up the mirror?

She can play on our team, she's good. She will run around everywhere and keep fighting!

Will she? How did they know that? Who told them?

She's fast! And fit! You can depend on her, she will always do her best to be there for you.

Who? Me? Yes! This was me. I would, I did, I do all those things. I just

LEFT: Permi Jhooti, who is now an artist, was the first British Asian professional footballer in the UK

I was the wrong colour, the wrong sex, the wrong, wrong, wrong

She saw me, would show me.

Football, sport, my tormentor. Let me count the ways in which you made it clear I was not on your team. I was the wrong colour, the wrong sex, the wrong, wrong, wrong.

The physical abuse, the mental and emotional abuse, it was wrong, wrong, wrong.

I do not want anyone to ever go through some of the things I did.

Yes. But.

I do not ever want to go back and take away my things I had to go through.

Football. The mirror it held up and the person it reflected back.

How would I ever have known who I was, the qualities I love that have brought me to this life I now lead?

I saw myself through sport. Any challenges I have ever faced in my life I can find an analogy within football. It always helps me find a way forward, gives me an answer. It provided me not just with beautiful moments, teammates and friends; it provided me a life and a philosophy that lives beyond the pitch.

Now, on those occasions I walk into a room, as the woman who proudly strides in, knowing she has a voice and a power, I look up over the heads, through the bodies of all those confident and loud voices, I look for you.

You are quieter than the others, have made yourself smaller, are hiding in the shadows. You are asking all those questions I once asked myself, yes?

But, I see you. ✖

Permi Jhooti is an artist, academic and former professional football player

51(03):80/81|DOI:10.1177/03064220221126443

hadn't considered what it meant. I liked the sound of this 'she'. This me.

Football. The first time I ever had a glimpse of who I may be, of what I may be able to contribute, if only I was given the opportunity; if I didn't have to take my place in the shadows. Football. The world which allowed me to give of myself, valued it, saw me.

It held up a mirror: take a good look at yourself, fix that image in your mind - this is you. Remember this when you go back out into that other world, the one in which the others just can't quite see.

You can have her.

No, it's OK, you can have her.

I keep my head down, don't look anyone in the eyes. I walk over to one of the teams, the one where maybe somewhere inside there is an ally, someone who knows me a little. Because that, that person they just witnessed, the unwanted outsider? That is not me, it cannot be me. Please, please, let that not be me.

Yes. But.

Football, sport, was my refuge no matter what was going on within me. On that pitch, or court or field, so much joy and freedom with the people who saw me - Justine, Daisy, Debbie and Tash. And Janet, my teacher, my coach, my mentor, my friend - the one who saw what I could be, should be, would be.

We don't like it – no one cares

Football fans around England are boycotting the World Cup out of principle, but is anyone listening to them asks **MARK GLANVILLE**?

ERIC CANTONA SAID of the 2022 football World Cup: "It's only about money. And the way they treated the people who built the stadiums, it's horrible. Personally, I will not watch it."

And now the great French footballer finds his sentiments echoed by many supporters of English football club Millwall, including once fanatical England follower Len Dussak.

"I can't be bothered watching England matches live or on TV," he said. "[Manager Gareth] Southgate and his politicising of the game haven't helped… We all know the score with [Qatar's] views on homosexuality and modern slavery, but still they go. I'd sooner remember when England meant something to me."

In a small but vocal corner of working-class support in an increasingly bourgeoisified game, Millwall fans (I'm one) thrive on their maverick "No one likes us" reputation. They received strong criticism when many booed the taking of the knee, Black Lives Matter's trademark gesture.

Millwall's boos were not motivated by racism. Tony Dolby, a lifelong Millwall supporter said: "Millwall fans have been kicking the s*** out of racists since the 70s when racism first reared its ugly head on the terraces. There are racist Millwall fans – there are racists in all walks of life – but we are not a racist club and never have been."

Millwall long ago subscribed to Kick it Out, football's anti-racist organisation – a move which has always been backed by the club's supporters. But fans were wary of BLM's political agenda and an attempt to burn the Union Flag on the cenotaph in 2020

PICTURED:
Political protest comes to the King Power Stadium, home of Leicester City FC

confirmed their suspicions. For working-class communities across the nation, commemorating those who died fighting for their country is a sacred duty.

Prominent in BLM UK were scions of the wealthy middle-class, the very types the Premier League likes to woo. Having already alienated many working-class supporters with tickets pricier than those for the opera, and having created an anodyne environment where swearing and standing are expellable offences, it was now cynically subscribing to a movement that spat in their faces.

Watching Southgate's England team continue to take the knee while happy to play in the Qatar World Cup increased their anger. In an apparent attempt to head off accusations of hypocrisy, Debbie Hewitt, England's Football Association chair, has explained that the competition provides "an opportunity to give the migrant workers a voice", and for players "to shine a light".

To quote two Millwall supporters: "If these c***s actually believed the s*** they preach, then we would not even go to the World Cup in Qatar.

"It's that simple, isn't it?"

The 2022 World Cup, born in blood and greed, has turned off countless fans, me included. Time to master the rules of American football. ✖

Mark Glanville is a writer and singer

> We all know the score with [Qatar's] views on homosexuality and modern slavery, but still they go

51(03):82/82|DOI:10.1177/03064220221126444

Much ado about critics

LYN GARDNER reacts to a theatre's threat towards unwelcome critics. Does being disinvited equate to being silenced?

THEATRES COURT CRITICS, even though they sometimes fear what they might write. The long-standing convention in theatreland is that critics are invited to press nights to review on a free ticket. There is always a risk that the reviews will be negative, but theatres are well aware that a slew of five-star raves can be box-office gold, and in these tough times they need all the help they can get. So, it's rare that theatres refuse to invite certain critics.

But that looked more likely to happen this summer after the notices appeared of a production of the musical Legally Blonde at the Regent's Park Open Air Theatre. Directed by Lucy Moss, the co-creator of sleeper musical success Six, the production featured a diverse cast of all shapes and sizes and considerable musical talent.

The Sunday Times theatre reviewer Quentin Letts responded to the production in a review in which one of the nicer lines declared: "The stage's superstructure wobbles under the weight of the company's loosely choreographed gyrations." The theatre hit back by issuing a statement that didn't mention Letts by name but referenced "the insensitive language of one review", and took a stand by saying that "we expect that everyone comments with respect and sensitivity, and those who decide not to will no longer be invited back to our theatre".

Critics being disinvited is not entirely new. Back in the 1960s, after a string of negative reviews, the Royal Court decided that Spectator critic Hilary Spurling was no longer welcome on press nights. Her colleagues on other titles stood shoulder to shoulder with her and said they would not review at the Court if Spurling were not invited.

ABOVE: The cast of Legally Blonde from Regent's Park Open Air Theatre, where one negative review sparked a backlash

Amidst talk of censorship and bans, the Arts Council threatened to remove its subsidy from the Court. Spurling's invitation was quickly reinstated.

Will a similar solidarity be shown towards Letts? Unlikely. The Open Air Theatre is unsubsidised, and a younger, more diverse group of critics in a profession which has long been dominated by white, middle-class Oxbridge-educated men see there is a significant difference between a critic taking issue with the artistic direction and output of a theatre (sometimes over a long period, as Spurling did) and cheap jibes and personal attacks on the physical appearance of performers.

In any case, there is a distinction between not being invited to review and being banned. When Letts was previously left off the guest list to review Kirstin Scott Thomas in The Audience, he simply bought a ticket.

I did the same when Cirque du Soleil decided one year that it did not want me reviewing its latest offering. Nobody stood at the door of the Royal Albert Hall and barred my entry. The Guardian still ran my thoughts about the show. My voice was not silenced, and I could and did write exactly what I wanted. Letts will continue to have the same right at the Open Air Theatre and other venues, whether he is invited or not. ✖

Lyn Gardner is associate editor at The Stage

> Nobody stood at the door of the Royal Albert Hall and barred my entry

51(03):83/83|DOI:10.1177/03064220221126445

On reputation laundering

The rich and powerful will use whatever means necessary to make themselves look good, writes **RUTH SMEETH**

THE RIGHT TO freedom of expression should be a straightforward concept to defend and promote. But life is never that easy, at least not in my experience. Even for Index's professional staff there are always debates to be had and lines to be considered. Something that we end up doing nearly every day.

What definition of free speech should we use? What is hate speech? Where is the line between defending freedom of expression and other core human rights? Where does context and nuance fit during an irrational debate? Who should have protected speech, if anyone? Does media freedom give journalists basic rights, or enhanced protections under Article 19? In a digital world where is the line on the right to speak versus the right to be heard? How do we ensure that freedom of speech is a protected right for everyone, not just those that can afford to take legal action? And then how do we stop people who can afford it from misusing the legal system to stifle debate in the public sphere? What is cancel

> How do we ensure that freedom of speech is a protected right for everyone, not just those that can afford to take legal action?

culture and is it a freedom of expression issue or a genuine method of protest, or both? What is academic freedom and how far should it and does it extend beyond the lecture hall? Where does the right to protest fall in these debates, if the protest itself undermines or attacks other people's freedom of expression?

Most importantly for me – what is the balance for Index between campaigning on many of the issues raised above versus providing a platform for dissidents who live under authoritarian rule, who without us and our campaigns would never be heard? When you're campaigning to protect people's rights to freedom of expression do you focus on those people who don't have any at all or do you seek to uphold the rights to freedom of speech for those that have already fought and won the battle?

In other words everything is a value judgement, even on an issue which on the surface should be as clear cut as it comes – the right to express yourself without fear or favour.

Index on Censorship seeks to balance all of these competing demands on our limited resources. We aim, every day, to provide a voice for the persecuted, using our platforms, including this magazine, to facilitate other people telling their stories when their government won't let them.

I am very aware, however, that the only reason Index gets to do this, online and off, is because of the protections we are afforded by living in a democracy, which is why we strive to protect those rights at home too. As Index's CEO my main priority is to ensure that the balance of our work doesn't become skewed and that the most important freedom of expression challenges facing

us – both at home and abroad – are the ones that we are focussing on.

This brings me to a recent conversation I had with my team. We were debating where we thought the next set of freedom of expression challenges would come from, both geographically and ideologically. If you're reading this edition of our magazine than you can imagine the conversation: next steps in Russian aggression; Chinese leader Xi Jinping's likely moves in the run-up to his 're-election' in October; increased hostility in the Balkans; the impact of the imminent election in Brazil and, of course, the on-going misery in the Middle East.

As the conversation developed we began discussing the current issue of the magazine and how some regimes seek to use global sport and the arts as a vehicle to "sportswash" or "creative wash" their global reputations. What became all too clear is that, as complex as Index's work programmes can be and as many issues as we now try and support, our work is actually now really split into three different areas:

1: First and foremost our work will always be to provide a platform for those dissident writers, scholars and artists who are being persecuted by authoritarian regimes

2: Campaigning to defend the core human right of freedom of expression, as outlined by Article 10 of the European Convention on Human Rights, both in the UK and in sister democracies.

3: Expose and challenge those state actors and individuals who seek to use their influence and the resources at their disposal to shape the narrative about them in the public space. In other words, expose 'reputation laundering'

Increasingly it's the third point which dominates my team's time and is something that's becoming increasingly prevalent in supposedly democratic countries. It's a concept now dominating my thoughts and dominating our approach to protecting freedom of expression.

Our extensive work opposing and exposing strategic lawsuits against public participation (SLAPPs), which are seemingly an increasingly common tool, when political figures and the uber wealthy use legal systems in democratic countries to tie up journalists and activists in overwhelming litigation to both bankrupt them and emotionally break them - this is clearly an effort to reputation launder.

Our work on Banned by Beijing falls into this category too. It exposes the efforts of the Chinese Communist Party to promote a version of Chinese culture and history which not only demands the Beijing line to be the dominant narrative outside of their own

borders but also attempts to promote an ethnically Han Chinese version of history and undermine Chinese diaspora communities when they seek to challenge the prevailing narrative determined by the CCP in their new home countries, especially in democratic states.

But China isn't the only nation-state engaging in this abuse of soft power. Increasingly we see similar tactics from Qatar, Russia, India and others.

And then we come to the very thorny issue of cancel culture, something that I spend an inordinate amount of time thinking about, especially when we consider what, if anything, Index should be doing in this space. When considered through the prism of reputation laundering could cancel culture be part of this trend? An effort to reshape our history, to delete the works of others in order to create a society or culture that works for you? All I can promise you is this; more on this area will follow as I get to grips with one of the most emotive aspects of our work. In the interim Index remains the voice for the persecuted.

Postscript

After writing this column the Index family watched in horror as news of the unsuccessful assasination attempt on Sir Salman Rushdie unfolded on our screens. Sir Salman was (and thankfully still is) the embodiment of the fight

> But China isn't the only nation-state engaging in this abuse of soft power. Increasingly we see similar tactics from Qatar, Russia, India and others

to protect and promote freedom of expression around the world. We are greatly indebted to him and his bravery as he refused, for decades, to be cowed by death threats and violence. His words and his art have cost him and his family a huge amount for over three decades. Today we are just grateful that he is still with us and our thoughts will be with him as he recovers from this horrendous attack. And I urge everyone of you to honour him and his work - by rereading his words and buying his books. ✖

Ruth Smeeth is CEO of Index

51(03):84/85|DOI:10.1177/03064220221126446

BELOW: A meeting between Russian President Vladimir Putin, Chinese President Xi Jinping and Brazilian President Jair Bolsonaro, men who go to extremes to control their country's reputation

CREDIT: Adriano Machado/Reuters/Alamy

HAY FESTIVAL

WINTER WEEKEND

24-27 NOVEMBER 2022

hayfestival.org/winterweekend

@HAYFESTIVAL #HAYWINTERWEEKEND

Castell Y Gelli
Hay Castle

Cymru
Wales

BAILLIE GIFFORD

Actual Investors

CULTURE

"You're just lying there like a rhino caught in some trap, rolling around in the mud. Look at yourself, how can you let such a rat play with you like this?"

STELLA GAITANO | EDO'S SOULS, P.88

The soul of Sudan

The award-winning South Sudanese writer **STELLA GAITANO** speaks to
KATIE DANCEY-DOWNS about being labelled a traitor for merely speaking up

STELLA GAITANO THINKS a lot about borders. They impact whether she's treated as a foreigner or a citizen, and she wonders who gets to make decisions on who stays and who is forced to leave.

Borders partly explain why she chooses to write in Arabic.

"There is a disconnect between north and south," explained Gaitano, who was born in Sudan where the official language is Arabic, to a South Sudanese family. She lost her citizenship after South Sudan became independent in 2011 and became stateless, forced to travel to South Sudan and get new documents, travelling through Kenya to avoid a closed border. This was the first of many experiences of displacement.

Part of the reason she writes in Arabic is to reach people who are being left out of the conversation. The people in Sudan weren't hearing about the injustices that those in South Sudan faced, because they were written about in English – also the language of intellectuals.

Gaitano's political activism was sparked at Khartoum University, while she was studying in the pharmacy faculty in order to break the chain of poverty weighing down her family. At first reluctant to get involved, Gaitano joined the student union. She attended street protests, spoke up for other students and discovered the power of changing people's lives. The government, she says, is afraid of these kinds of groups.

When Gaitano was forced to move to South Sudan, she knew both countries faced the same challenges – poor healthcare, marginalisation, poverty and lack of education, for starters.

"I knew there was marginalisation everywhere. I wanted to speak up for all of Sudan," she told Index. "I was writing about the problems and corruption people face even after independence."

When war started again in 2013, she remembers seeing the pain of it in people's eyes. Her desire to speak up for both Sudan and South Sudan landed her in trouble, firmly labelled as the writer who didn't want South Sudan to be independent. Whenever she had an article published, she was met with fury on social media and in the press.

At one publication where she was a contributor, her colleagues turned against her, posting screenshots on social media from a documentary in which she was upset, alongside degrading comments. At another, security (which she believes to be government sanctioned) made threats of closing the newspaper if Gaitano kept writing, telling her to use certain words over others and to dispense with her direct tone. She backed down to protect her colleagues.

When asked if the government or authorities ever tried to pressure her into silence, Gaitano said it was never direct.

"They put me in a place where I couldn't contribute," she said. "I don't know why it is happening. But suddenly

> Part of the reason she writes in Arabic is to reach people who are being left out of the conversation

I found that I can't write in South Sudan or even write issues relating to South Sudan. It pained me a lot. Really, they destroyed my heart."

And then, Gaitano said, she gave up.

In 2015, she returned once again to Sudan, after activist journalists were targeted and the situation became worse for her in South Sudan. But while she was in the north, she had to keep quiet. A revolution three years later allowed her to work again. She visited camps for internally displaced people and opened libraries in marginalised areas.

But her relative freedom was short-lived. A military coup in 2021 changed Sudan, and for Gaitano it ended with threats and another hostile environment for writing. The timing couldn't have been more perfect for an invitation from PEN Germany to join the writers-in-exile programme there for three years.

For the first time in many years, Gaitano feels safe to write freely. She has settled into writing her next novel, a continuation of Edo's Souls (which won an award from PEN). An extract from Edo's Souls is published exclusively below.

In this book, Gaitano documents the life of a character – the connection to her culture, her environment and her community. "[The characters] are really connected to that village, that has the deep, deep African culture, and how people are dealing with their daily life," she explained. "And then, when they are forced to go, I think it is like the experience of me or my mother or most South Sudanese [people], when they are

CREDIT: (inset) Doha Mohammed; (right) Eva Bee

ABOVE: South Sudanese writer Stella Gaitano

forced to leave their lands, and what they can do with all this backup of culture."

Gaitano's books are not banned in South Sudan, where the government perhaps underestimates the impact of fiction. Journalism, however, might be a different story, with criticism being more direct. As for Sudan, the government wants to know exactly what is written, fiction or otherwise.

In countries facing political unrest and discrimination, Gaitano believes stories play a major role, especially when the writer has political awareness about the country, the system and the behaviour of its leaders.

Now, in Germany, she can turn her mind from thoughts of only "north" and "south". She meets people from around the whole world, sharing stories and finding similarities.

"Now, I have my own borders."

Katie Dancey-Downs is assistant editor at Index

51(03):88/91|DOI:10.1177/03064220221126449

Edo's Souls

AT DAWN ONE day, Edo stopped by Rebecca Ilaygha's because they had arranged to gather wood together. Rebecca was a short, full woman: a tree stump with luminescent ebony skin and an infectious laugh always accompanied by tears. Edo found her drying the water out from sprouting maize: honey-coloured water dripping onto the dirt courtyard now hard with compacted layers of silt and manure as Rebecca forced her six children to kneel down and lap up the maize-infused water, the way livestock do from puddles. While they did so she moistened her broom with the same liquid and beat them on their bottoms, convinced that all this was the cure for wetting themselves, having tried every herb and root under the sun to no avail.

Edo came with an astonishing idea. She advised her to fasten toads round their waists: the creatures' racket would keep the children awake and they'd have no choice but to go outside to relieve themselves. Rebecca cackled and said she was out of her mind, but in the end she tried it, smacked with despair. Rebecca caught six toads from the swamp and tied them round the children's middles amidst their screams, with Edo's help herself, as the orchestrator. Their mother sent them to bed, shuddering from having such creatures stuck to them, even though she herself couldn't sleep what with the toads croaking and her children crying, until daybreak approached and complete quiet settled in the room. Exhausted, the little ones fell asleep and the toads fell silent, squashed under the worn out bodies, their tongues hanging and excrement oozing out.

In the morning the reed mat was dry and the dirt floor of the room wasn't decorated with moist designs anymore. Rebecca removed the flattened toads from the children's waists and sent them to pass water, their bladders almost bursting from the accumulated urine. Some scratched for several days with rashes all over from the toads' poisonous secretions, and from that day forward they never wet themselves again.

Other mothers imitated Rebecca in this matter and after a short while it became something they all did, but no one knew that it had been Edo's idea all along; Rebecca never revealed as much to anyone and it was one of the many reasons why their friendship was so strong. Rebecca, who then became the wet nurse to her only daughter.

Edo's other friend Marta Isai was the most battered woman in the village; everyone was accustomed to her wailing and she, accustomed to the beatings – her bones warped due to fractures she had neglected to set straight, her body a map of cicatrices and her features always hard to make out through the bruises, even though she was a statuesque, fleshy woman as solid as an ancient citadel and her husband was an entire three meters shorter than her, the vile drunkard that he was. They never had any children and so Marta, crippled with guilt, bore the beatings claiming that she deserved them. After one of the nights where Marta had been howling and weeping, her husband abusing her with the foulest of words, painting her infertile and lesbian, her ass as barren as they come, Edo stopped by. Her friend was crumpled on the reed mat like a diseased rhino, ribs probably cracked, spitting blood. Furious with what had become of her neighbour, Edo scoffed, 'You just can't get enough, can you? Don't you know how powerful you are? You're just lying there like a rhino caught in some trap, rolling around in the mud. Look at yourself, how can you let such a rat play with you like this? Breaking your bones every day and giving you new bruises?'

'What can I do?'

Edo picked up the thick cane that he beat her with; her eyes travelled up and down the length of it like a customer appraising its quality. 'Beat

Don't you know how powerful you are? You're just lying there like a rhino caught in some trap

him,' she determined.

'Beat him?' Marta bit her lip. 'Can a woman even beat a man? No, no, it'd be too much of a disgrace and I'd be the talk of the village.'

'Are you safe from their tongues now? People are going to always talk, why not change what they're talking about and make it more thrilling? More strange?'

'But he'd kill me!'

'You're already dead, because a man like that will slit your throat like you're some sick goat, claiming that you're useless. He thinks that he's wasted his cows and sheep in a marriage that didn't do what it's supposed to.'

Marta grew tense to the point she started coughing and spit out a sticky red lump of blood.

Edo calmly placed the cane down, letting it point to the lump of bodily matter knitted with threads of blood. 'In any case it's up to you.' She gazed out the door, her eyes glowing as the sun rays began to cast shadows. 'People's tongues were made to blab. They must be going on and on about how a rhino like yourself let a small frog like him play with you this way, someone like him whose had all his feathers plucked out. And how maybe, his third leg doesn't even have the water of life to give you a child in the first place.' Trying to keep a straight face she added, 'Stupid woman.' Then she slipped away, as soundless as a snake.

Marta started to stare at the red sticky lump and her crooked bones. Anger roiled within. She grabbed the cane, its thickness filling her palm, her eyes reduced to slits and inhaled deeply. She held it behind her heaving weary body, her heart beat racing, her chest swiftly rising and falling. Hot air escaped from deep within and several muscles in her face and body twitched; thick grains of sweat pooled atop her nose and forehead, then slowly slid down like raindrops.

That evening her husband came home and started misbehaving with her, insulting her, complaining about all the cattle he had lost in paying her dowry. He said that he was going to kill her, slice her up, and feed her to flying and crawling critters, all the while kicking her in the stomach. She swiftly rose up before him like a tree breaking forth from the depths of the earth,

When he'd beat me every night why didn't any of you come save me?

standing in the middle of the room, in the exact stance she would use when chopping wood with her axe, her legs firmly spread apart, the cane heavy in her palms; she crashed down upon him with all her pent up frustration, beating, beating, beating him – each time the cane would make contact, she whacked him so fiercely that his mother, his family, his ancestors felt it. Panting, her insults fell into rhythm with her blows.

Thwack - you son of a –

Thwack - you dirty –

When he broke out into a wail as a woman would, she dragged him outside to the courtyard for everyone to see, and with one hand she picked him up, tossed him up in the air, and flung him down to the ground, again and again; she then beat him with the cane as one threshes maize, till he lost consciousness and she sat atop him heaving a sigh like a wild animal.

Some men tried to approach to free her husband from her grip but she pointed the cane at them, her breaths staccato, 'If you get any closer, someone's going to die. When he'd beat me every night why didn't any of you come save me? Was he beating a dead animal skin? If any of you have an itch and need me to beat it out of you, do come closer.' The ring of onlookers broke up, rolling back as rings of water do when you toss a pebble in.

Breathing heavily like an agitated bull, Marta spewed bloody mucus out at great distances. She had stretched out and expanded till she resembled her *gutiyyah* in size, transforming into a huge mass of agitation, her eyes as wide as they would go.

Her two friends Edo and Rebecca drew close to her, each of them grabbing an arm. Grinning so widely in the darkness that her golden tooth flashed, Edo whispered, 'Good for you!' ✖

Extracted from Stella Gaitano's book Edo's Souls,
translated by Sawad Hussain

Moving the goalposts

KAYA GENÇ tells **GUILHERME OSINSKI** about the link between football and politics, and the climate that led to his new short story, which is published here

AFTER YEARS OF President Reccep Erdoğan chipping away at freedoms in Turkey, Kaya Genç is concerned that even if his rule ends, rights might not recover.

"I'm worried that this psychological assault - conducted through Erdoğan's media empire, which includes CNN's Turkish edition which is the most passionate defender of the autocratic regime - may succeed."

We're talking to Genç in light of his short story written and published below, which fictionalises an infamous football match organised in Istanbul before the 2014 presidential elections, in order to boost Erdoğan's popularity among the electorate. Erdoğan was prime minister then; he wore a jersey numbered "12"; it was a fixed match, a "show" for audiences. A fortnight later Erdoğan became the 12th president of Turkey.

"Football and politics are the two most important things in Turkey," said the journalist and Index contributor. In his words, football is a platform where people feel they can make their voices heard. In recent years, however, as this incidents shows, football has become politicised and controlled.

"The government has decided to contain this issue, by introducing a surveillance system with a special card and a seat assigned to you", said Genç.

"If a camera catches you chanting against the government, they might knock at your door or the police take you away," he said.

This has led to people self-censoring.

"Everyone seems very muted."

Even so, Genç says football fans haven't stopped singing against the ruthless government led by Erdoğan.

"Suddenly you hear chants from the stadiums about a commander in the Ottoman army who rebelled against the monarchy and started a revolution. So everyone knows it's a message to the government."

In April 2017, a constitutional referendum took place in Turkey and the parliamentary system gave way to an executive presidency and a presidential system. More than five years on, Genç talks about a coalition of opposition parties that today offers a way out for Turkey. It brings hopes that people can regain their freedom. But Genç is afraid of the fear Erdoğan has spread across Turkey in case his government falls.

Another point of concern is the relationship between Turkey and Russia.

"Opportunism, not principles, guides Ankara's relationship with Moscow. Sadly, the Turkish foreign ministry has tilted the country's axis to illiberal regimes, and, is firmly aligning Turkey with Russia and former Soviet autocracies, instead of Brussels and Washington."

Guilherme Osinski is editorial assistant at Index

51(03):92/95|DOI:10.1177/03064220221126450

CREDIT: Studiostoks

Defender of the Faith

THE PRIME MINISTER is coming to the game. That's what my teammates say. Not to watch, but to play. In just two weeks, he'll have his big day, I say. With the presidential elections just around the corner, what's he doing, spending precious time kicking balls with the likes of us? Perhaps, my teammates say, he wants to score a goal or two, that famed former player who exchanged football for power. In front of an audience, they say, the autocrat shall show some of his tricks, and that's good before the polling day before he's crowned emperor. He's coming to our stadium tomorrow, I tell myself, and I'm the goalie, and when my teammates ask what I'll do when our leader approaches me with a ball in his foot and a determined look in his eye, I stay mum. Whether I'll let him score is my business, I say.

It's July 26, a humid day, and we're under the spotlights, as we often are. Eighteen thousand people are watching from the stands. Eight state-of-the-art cameras are buzzing around, filming our movements in HD: Spidercams, Jimmy Jibs, all that high-tech crap. Spectators speak in different voices tonight. They're chanting "One nation! One flag! One homeland! One state! One chief!" as if in a German book-burning rally from 1933. They're singing: "Chief! Chief! You lead! We follow!"

I fail to get politics. I get it when spectators shout: "Referee, pussy referee, oh referee, pussy referee!" or scream, "Blind, this referee is, blind, this referee iiiis!" All those rhymes are rooted in frustrations about our beautiful game. But politics is all sham: how can people devote their lives to them, I say. Still, my wife swears it's part of the job—we're just players in games designed by others, she says. Play along. Play along, honey. It's just a game, a game.

But I'm not just a player, I sneer, I'm a defender, and I need to, and I shall defend as much as I can.

The roar is deafening. The prime minister's son-in-law is running in circles. Suave, American-educated, he's in my team. Dressed in white like me, he is standing next to me, that bright man with a future role in the prime minister's "A-team." These conservatives are all snobs, I notice, even more so when they showily play "the people's game" or shake a poor man's hand.

"Our white jersey may be an advantage," I propose to Reza. "They're named the 'White Party,' no?" My friend, the now-retired football legend, will play forward with us tonight, and he inspects my words like a field commander mulling over a map. No, he mumbles in a dreadful tone, "white was what they claimed to be, you see. Fifteen years ago is now ancient history. Today, white equals 'white Turks', the elites! We're the arrogance of 'white Europe,' which they'll need to publicly screw for votes. All the 'black Turks' today will wish death to thee."

Not well-versed in sociology, I stare at him blankly. We pee together, exchanging observations, and comparing stratagems. "I'll go easy on them," muses Reza as I struggle not to stain my underwear with the last drop, hopelessly defending its whiteness. "And you shall let the chief score goals, kiddie."

The prime minister's team, dressed in orange, materialises like lions on a colosseum. That's the colour of their party, and he's wearing a jersey numbered 12—a reference to next month's elections. If elected, the former ball kicker will be Turkey's twelfth president, you see.

*

I'm a man who likes to play by the rules. We don't have in football a Hippocratic oath, but I do profess one: *primum non fallere*. First, do not cheat. →

The prime minister's team, dressed in orange, materialises like lions on a colosseum

→ My dad used to take us to the sea when I was a kid and when he was alive, where he allowed me to swim away from the sureties of the beach. Under one condition: "As long as you're careful in the depths, son, there'll be nothing to fear." So he gave me freedom, and my mom's protestations disappeared like vanishing sands.

I'd follow his rules at all times. Swim into depths and rotate back when it feels dangerous. Bike on my lane and use the horn and signal before turns because that is what's right—a lifelong habit of following rules, not leaders.

Dead and casketed for years now, he watches me, I see.

"Crush them! Crush them! Just give the order, and we'll crush vandals of Gezi, crush the vandals of Gezi!" The chant appals and infuriates, and I remember our time at Gezi Park last year with my wife and sister-in-law, when we watched activists, those brave souls, singing songs and lighting bonfires. Defenders like me of goals others desired to prey on.

I watch the son of the prime minister. A different sort of character. Sprinting on the field, playing with his old man. Behind him, a chubby man, newly tasked with buying off Freedom and Nationhood, two mainstream papers, once so critical, now servile to their bone.

The crony's rumoured not to have read a single book his entire life. Proud of that, I suppose. Loyal and servile, he's a winner in their New Turkey.

The Istanbul head of the ruling party is there, too, cracking jokes with a basketball star. Photographers, having a field day, snap frantically. Spent 15 seasons in the NBA, played for Orlando Magic, Toronto Raptors and Los Angeles Clippers, and is now an adviser to the prime minister. Not where I dream of ending up. Next to them stands Turkey's most incredible living football legend, his moniker, the Devil.

Reza's great opponent in the past, the Devil, is playing for the orange team tonight. I hear the whistle and a rising roar from the stands: "Say die, die, and we all die! We all die for you, oh Chief, we all die for you, oh Chief!"

I hear the whistle and a rising roar from the stands: "Say die, die, and we all die! We all die for you, oh Chief, we all die for you"

I sense a heaviness around me and hear a precept issued by unseen forces. It demands me to disappear, to comply. During the kick off, Reza tosses a coin with the prime minister, and I watch the dime whirl around and drop with a clink. Reza smiles and courtesies towards the prime minister, who smiles before kickstarting this game.

He passes the ball to Devil, who delivers it to the prime minister's chubby crony. Accustomed to spending his time on Instagram chasing women and drinking bourbon on his yacht, the poor man cannot carry the ball and soon collapses. A distant applause rises when the bearded son-in-law takes the ball from his foot and passes it to Reza, who shoots it with such impeccable skill that we score tonight's first goal.

Silence in the stadium. What reporters must be feeling the mornings they expose state secrets? Panicked executives ponder possibilities at the bench. The linesman, a deadly expression on his face, his hand on his heart, in pain for having rebelled. Players in orange jerseys turn to him confrontationally, expecting an offside whistle, at the least. He's frozen, his arms refusing to rise, for there was no offside, you see, and he's made a career of following rules until this moment. Now the prime minister is running to him, shouting that the goal was unfair. "Hear the nation's will! Hear their chants! Nobody can resist the will of our nation! Know your place, white Turk!" The referee whistles promptly, and the goal is cancelled in the name of "advanced democracy". Players must continue as if the previous five minutes were but a dream.

His mood boosted by the decision—always, always good to be on the winners' team! — the NBA player approaches the centre circle and makes a back pass to the prime minister, who crosses the ball as the Devil attempts a dummy run. But it's the prime minister who gallops between our midfielders and comes perilously close to my castle.

After a brief pause, he hoofs—the ball, surprisingly fast, approaches my goal post, like an inevitable historical event, the Fall of the Berlin Wall, and yet I interfere, I jump and catch it, I defend my home.

The prime minister, disappointed and furious, feels his throne is in peril. Silence among spectators soothes my soul. I goal kick; as the ball leaves the goal line, frustrated executives point in my direction, shouting in each other's ears: oh, that mad boy, the usurper of people's will!

The son-in-law kicks the ball. With a brisk sprint, he back-passes it to another small-time crony who, unusually fit, starts hugging the line while another "businessman", who gets all our government's hospital tenders, defends him. That man's ancestors had taken over several properties of a Greek family in Istanbul, I know ("squatted on them" as we say in Turkish, a language so rich with words about such robberies!) thanks to their steadfast loyalty to the Turkish state. Now at loggerheads with the orange team, a nasty foul fells him on the ground.

The young crony screams obscenities, and boos rise from the stands. "Get up, stand up, stand up for your Chief!"

The prime minister orders the fighting duo to make up—bad press otherwise. And so his adaptable allies hug like old lovers, shaking hands, whispering niceties. Still, there is a free kick. I see a wall formed outside the penalty area, and the header by Reza hits the crossbar leading to a corner kick. Watching them, I leave my castle momentarily when the prime minister spots a chance. Taking the ball, he passes the centre circle, attempting a chip shot. I jump high and punch his rubber gift and hear another boo from the stands.

* * *

Kick off. The second half begins. Reza, that football wizard, steals the ball from the prime minister's son, which leaves the young Islamic entrepreneur in tears. I have failed, oh father, I have failed you so badly! Half a minute later, Reza scored another goal which the referee again cancelled. This time, no need to hear from the prime minister. His instincts have turned into our rules.

I remain proud of my clean sheet. The other goalie conceded twice, despite cancellations, never shall I be guided by rules other than football's. The match extends into extra time, and in a moment of confusion, the son-in-law trips up the NBA player who falls to his face near the goal-post.

I hear the distant voices of commentators and coaches, and spectators sitting in bars as the Chief warms up for his penalty kick. Last orders, I hear, last chance for this once flourishing goalie. Then I hear my wife begging me to play ball, and I hear Reza, "don't be proud, it's a sin, kiddie, it's a sin." But a sin is when we acquiesce under fear, and I see this light in the air, and my father descends from the heavens to say: "Just play it by the rules, son, and what relief thou shall feel."

The prime minister reaches the penalty spot and kicks the ball. Our freedoms on the precipice, our justice hanging by a thread, it's coming, the football, and I punch with all my might this oppressive offering outside the pitch, outside the border of my being, outside what I see today, so that I can face tomorrow, that terrifying thing, with some self-respect. The ball spins like a fortune's wheel, and it disappears into a future where my child may thank me for doing the right thing when the assault was real and the repercussions severe.

"Arrest the goalie! Arrest the goalie!" roars the stadium in unison. I raise my fist triumphantly, the defender of the faith of rule-followers, a world champion, naive perhaps, but at least, free. ✖

Kaya Genç is a novelist and contributing editor at Index. He is based in Istanbul

END NOTE

Away from the satanic

Rushdie's attack warns of a less tolerant world, but hope is coming from an unlikely corner, writes **MALISE RUTHVEN**

THE ATTACK ON Salman Rushdie is a grim reminder of a sad contemporary reality. If a writer can be assaulted and stabbed, in full public view, in the pleasant surroundings of Chautauqua in bucolic upstate New York, is anywhere safe for the free exchange of ideas? Rushdie's satirical novel The Satanic Verses, based on a story that the devil had tried to insert an idolatrous passage into the Koran, the sacred text of Islam, caused outrage throughout the Muslim world when it appeared in 1988. The culprit in the recent New York attack may have acted independently but there can be no doubt that he was inspired by the 1989 fatwa issued by Iranian leader Ayatollah Khomeini, which demanded Rushdie's execution as an apostate following the publication of his book.

Rushdie's survival since 1989 is a glimmer of hope in a darkening scene. A Pew Research Centre survey found that in 2019, 79 countries – 40% of the 198 studied – had blasphemy laws, outlawing anything thought to slight religion. A survey in 2013 found that 62% of people in Malaysia, 86% in Egypt and 76% in Pakistan favoured the execution of apostates who desert the Islamic faith.

In Iran, members of the minority Bahá'í Faith, who are accused of being apostates, are now being rendered homeless, with their houses bulldozed by the regime. Even where laws against blasphemy do not exist, lampooning religion can lead to death at the hands of those who see themselves as executing God's will, as was seen with the Charlie Hebdo attack in France.

In an era of multiculturalism, populism and heightened sensitivities about sexuality, belief and identity, the road to tolerance and reason is becoming ever more perilous.

There remain, however, small filaments of hope. The Pew survey suggested that the younger generation were less religiously observant and less judgmental than their parents.

Societies long exposed to secular regimes show much lower levels of approval for laws against blasphemy and apostasy, despite signs of growing intolerance in online culture wars where activists seek to cancel their opponents. There may also be a small and stony footpath to reason in the work of Muslim scholars in Western universities, such as Ahab Bdaiwi of Leiden and the late Shahab Ahmed of Harvard.

Ahmed, who died in 2015 aged 48, showed in Before Orthodoxy – The Satanic Verses in Early Islam how painstaking academic research can unpack the myths that sustain populist feeling. After examining the earliest sources, Ahmed found a widespread and untroubled consensus on the historical authenticity of The Satanic Verses episode, which stood in marked contrast to the doctrinally orthodox rejection of the story that emerged in later centuries. His work provides an abundance of data that could be deployed to challenge Rushdie's caricature of a divine emissary who instructs the faithful in the mundane details of life, by spouting "rules, rules, rules".

Ahmed and Bdaiwi's research is consistent with the work of other Muslim intellectuals such as Turkish writer Mustafa Aykol, who laments the closing of Muslim minds via the dominance of legal proscriptions.

Such work may take time to reach the inner recesses of a piety constructed around outdated gender distinctions and rigid behavioural norms. But the signposts are clearly marked. ✖

Malise Ruthven is the author of Islam in the World, A Satanic Affair - Salman Rushdie and the Wrath of Islam and other books

---

BELOW: Award-winning author Salman Rushdie in New York in 2016

CREDIT: Orjan Ellingvag/Alamy

51(03):96/96|DOI:10.1177/03064220221126453